CONGRESS:
AMERICA'S PRIVILEGED CLASS

H. Lon Henry

Prima Publishing
P.O. Box 1260BK
Rocklin, CA 95677
(916) 786-0426

To my grandaughters, Ashleigh and Maren, in the fond hope this book will help bring into their lives a government of the people, which truly represents all the people.

© 1994 by H. Lon Henry

Composition by Professional Book Center
Production by Andi Reese Brady
Copyediting by Becky Whitney
Cover Design by The Dunlavey Studio, Sacramento
Cover illustration by Michael Witte

Library of Congress Cataloging-in-Publication Data
Henry, H. Lon
    Congress, America's privileged class / H. Lon Henry
        p. cm.
    Includes index
    ISBN 1-55958-459-9 : $6.95
    1. United States. Congress—Salaries, etc. 2. United States.
Congress—Salaries, etc.—History.   I. Title.
JK781.H46 1993
328.73'0733—dc20   9323549
                                                        CIP

How to order:

Single copies may be ordered from Prima Publishing, P.O. Box 1260BK, Rocklin, CA 95677; telephone (916) 786-0426. Quantity discounts are also available. On your letterhead, include information concerning the intended use of the books and the number of books you wish to purchase.

94 95 96 97 RRD 10 9 8 7 6 5 4 3 2 1

Printed in the United States of America

CONTENTS

Preface

"People seldom improve when they have no other model
but themselves to copy after." —*Oliver Goldsmith*

In an egalitarian body like Congress, where personal
influence is the operative mechanism, there will inevita-
bly emerge a pattern of individual self-interest prevailing
over the collective responsibility. Self-interest is the natural end product of a political system that in virtually
every way exalts individual self-aggrandizement over party
and institutional responsibility.

This outward manifestation of individual self-interest is
expressed as *privilege,* which is defined by the *Living Webster Encyclopedic Dictionary* as, "a right, immunity, or benefit enjoyed by a particular person or a restricted group of
persons beyond the common advantages of others . . ."
The United States Congress, in its egregious preoccupa-
tion with all things self-serving, has developed privileges
of epic proportion.

Whatever privilege Congress grants itself is ultimately
paid for by the beleaguered United States taxpayers.
Unable individually to redress the inequities of big gov-

ernment, taxpayers vote into office a champion to represent their interests in Washington and then despairingly
watch that champion become one of the enemy.

The old adage that "power corrupts, and absolute
power corrupts absolutely" is exemplified to its fullest in
our capital city. There, the Congress is unchallenged in
its control of the nation's purse strings and imperiously
rules over its own actions, which promotes pervasive and
perpetual corruption in government while insidiously
rigging the political system to guarantee lifetime job tenure. Congress has become cavalier in rewarding itself
every conceivable privilege, indulgence, and exemption.
Congress is employed for the benefit and convenience of
its individual members, certainly not for any larger purpose.

Congressional privilege is again under public attack
because of excessive and unconscionable abuses by members. Already some perks have been jettisoned, and congressional leaders are being privately warned that other
privileges are in danger of being axed. The scandals are
taking their toll, and, for now at least, lawmakers can no
longer put off or ignore debts owed to their private restaurant, use congressional staffers to get their parking
tickets fixed, or kite a check at their private bank.

Despite current public outrage, prevailing wisdom dic-
tates that, after the furor diminishes, it will be back to
business as usual. According to consumer advocate Ralph
Nader, "The motto on Capitol Hill is, if you can get it,
grab it." Although some minor sacrifices may yet be
made to quell taxpayer indignation, no program of
bicameral reform is in place to curtail this pattern of
excessive, individual self-indulgence.

Perhaps this book will spur the reform process by
informing the American public of the magnitude of congressional abuse. A public uninformed about the myriad
unseen and unwarranted benefits and privileges enjoyed
by members of Congress at taxpayers' expense is a public

handicapped in the exercise of its responsibilities in the voting booth. This first condition must be corrected if we are to redress intelligently the latter.

Americans have a deep-seated antipathy toward anything that smacks of special privileges for the favored few. Although some of the services available to members of Congress are necessary for them to effectively carry out their official duties and responsibilities, the majority grossly exceed those provided to the average working American and must be dispensed with if public outrage is to be extinguished.

Only when every member of Congress understands that public trust requires an effective and accountable legislative body devoting its energy and interest to what really matters—the unsolved problems on the nation's agenda—will the public's perception of Congress as a personal plaything for its members be eliminated.

ACKNOWLEDGMENTS

Congress: America's Privileged Class would not have been possible without the help of countless individuals and institutions. An investigative journal is never popular with those being investigated, so cooperation from those within that select circle was virtually non-existent. And because Congress in its infinite wisdom had seen fit to exempt itself from the Freedom of Information Act, walking down that avenue was a trip to nowhere.

Two notable exceptions to the silent treatment were the cooperation of the office of freshman Congressman Randy "Duke" Cunningham, whose staff was instrumental in obtaining information from the Library of Congress, and the office of Senator Charles Grassley, whose office lent information concerning congressional exemptions.

Numerous organizations and institutions provided documents, correspondence, oral history, and written material of every description. Althought it is not possible to thank the individuals associated with each organization, I would like to express my gratitude to the following institutions: the National Taxpayers Union; Congress Watch; Citizens Against Government Waste; Congressional Reform; Common Cause; Congressional Accountability; and the Center for Study of Responsive Law; the United States Library of Congress; the San Diego Public Library; The University of Southern California (The Doheny Library); and the University of California at San Diego Library.

Among the agencies of government who provided assistance were the National Capital Planning Commission; Architect of the Capitol; House Committee on the District of Columbia; Washington Convention and Visitors Association; District of Columbia Chamber of Commerce; and the office of the Librarian to the Library of Congress.

I am especially indebted to investigative reporters throughout the country, whose diligence, persistence, and skill gleaned those numerous facts and figures not readily available to an author on a limited budget. It is important to recognize the various publications on whose pages were reported the many small bits and pieces of information that contributed so much to the whole picture. Notable among these were the *Los Angeles Times*, the *Washington Post*, the *San Diego Union Tribune*, the *San Francisco Chronicle*, the *New York Times*, the *Wall Street Journal*, the *Garden Island Press*, *Time* magazine, and *Readers Digest*.

My ultimate love and gratitude go to the ladies in my life: Beverly, Myrtle, Laura, Ashleigh, Maren, and to my son, Drake, without whose encouragement and forbearance this book would not have been written.

1

The Perks and Privileges of Rank

It is fair to state that many of the congressional perks and privileges enjoyed by today's lawmakers were born of necessity during the early days (circa 1867) of Congress in Washington, D.C. Back then the Capitol, isolated from the center of Washington, could be reached only by a long ride over muddy streets. The majority of lawmakers were forced to live in boarding houses, mostly without indoor baths or conveniences. Eating out was inconvenient and considered by many to be hazardous to their health.

Over the years Congress has proven more than equal to the task of improving its conditions. Ever conscious of its prestigious position and general welfare, it has now amassed a broad array of benefits and perquisites (perks) for senators, House members, and their staffs that enables them to live in the nation's capital in a relatively fine, if not opulent, style.

Problems with perks arise when lawmakers, never content with moderation, abuse their privileges. For example, few people begrudge government-provided postage "for official business," known as the congressional "frank" (the privilege of mailing unlimited pieces of mail to constituents at taxpayers' expense). In addition to providing incumbents with a tremendous campaign advantage, however, franking privileges cost taxpayers a staggering $89.5 million in 1989, and the House "frank" alone cost taxpayers nearly $73 million in 1990.

Abuse of the franking privilege has been so great in the past—members have mailed their laundry, china, and bedding, and in one case even mailed a horse—that both the House and the Senate are reported to be again revising the franking guidelines to include stricter accounting procedures and limits on the amount of mail Congress can send to its constituents.

A perk is defined as *something additional to regular profit or pay, resulting from one's position or employment, especially something customary or expected like a tip or gratuity. It is a privilege or benefit to which a person or institution is entitled by virtue of status, position, or the like: a perogative.**

A perk ceases to be an advantage or a benefit when it is perceived as unwarranted, unnecessary, or abuse of privilege. Congress takes great pains to keep the public in the dark about the many benefits and privileges it enjoys at taxpayers' expense. However, public outrage has turned many a perk into a liability after congressional abuse forced it into the spotlight.

The allowances and services available to members of Congress are outlined in the U.S. House of Representatives *Congressional Handbook* and its Senate equivalent. Commonly referred to as the "Green Book" because of its green binder, it is generally unavailable to members of the public. It is one of the first items provided to freshmen members of Congress, who are encouraged by senior members to make use of the benefits described

---

* Source: The Congressional Accountability Project Report on Pay and Perks.

therein to the fullest extent possible. After all, the freshmen are now members of the most exclusive club in the world and should fully enjoy everything attendant to their new position.

Many of the benefits discussed in this chapter—benefits out of reach of the ordinary citizen—are taken from the Green Book and are representative of the dozens of taxpayer-supported perquisites members of Congress have enjoyed for years.

Because Congress exempts itself from the Freedom of Information Act and for obvious reasons is not enthusiastic about cooperating with a book of this nature, it is not possible to guarantee that every perk has been listed. However, thanks to the energies of numerous private organizations and citizens' watchdog groups, plus the efforts of private reporting agencies willing to share their data, it is safe to assume that most perks (certainly the more egregious) have been included.

The following are not presented in any particular priority, although some effort has been made to group like items in the same general area.

MEDICAL SERVICES

The Office of the Attending Physicians Service, traditionally a Navy doctor with a staff of other doctors, nurses, and medical technologists, is located in the Capitol to address the special needs of the lawmakers. The office was established in 1928, when members were dying at an alarming rate, many apparently from diseases related to the capital environment—a condition not evident today.

This office dispenses free medical advice and prescription pharmaceuticals to lawmakers only. Specialized services include a medical response team; ambulance service; a complete medical laboratory, x-ray, and pharmacy service; free medical tests; free blood; and free immunization and allergy injections. Additionally, for a $400 (formerly $100) annual fee, senators and their employees may use the Senate Health Club fitness centers, including a private gym where they can use the swimming pools and weight rooms and receive massages. The recent public outrage over congressional perks forced Congress to impose a $520 annual fee on members who continue to use the services of the Capitol physician. This fee is in addition to the charges now paid by members for private health insurance. This fee, however, is substantially less than the $652 deductible that Medicare users are required to pay each benefit period.

God forbid you should suffer a medical misfortune while visiting the Capitol, because you would be shocked to learn that you are not entitled to treatment, even emergency services, at the Office of the Attending Physicians Service. It's strictly for members only—ordinary citizens need not apply, even though it is paid for by your tax dollars.

INSURANCE BENEFITS

Additionally, all members of Congress are eligible to participate in the Federal Employees Health program.

A basic life-insurance policy for $99,000 is provided to all members of the House of Representatives, and senators receive basic life insurance of $101,000. Taxpayers pick up one-third of the premium costs.

HOUSING BENEFITS

Members of Congress have not neglected themselves when it comes to housing. They voted themselves a special tax deduction of up to $3,000 per year for living expenses while they're away from their congressional district or home state.

COMFORTS AWAY FROM HOME

To make life more enjoyable while in Washington serving their constituencies from afar, Congress has prescribed themselves a number of painkillers. The following list describes many privileges members of Congress feel are essential to doing their job without undue stress:

- Special orange **license plates permit parking virtually anywhere** in the District of Columbia "while on business." Until recently, if a House member received a ticket (double-parking outside a Washington night spot at 2 A.M., for example), the House Sergeant At Arms would get it "fixed" for him. Now, however, he has to get it fixed by a personal staff member.
- **Free parking** at special parking lots located next to the terminals at Washington National and Dulles airports and the Union Rail Station is provided to members of Congress. What if members of Congress need a ride home from the airport? They just charge the taxi fare to the Federal Deficit.
- Each representative and senator is provided with **one free garage space** for personal use. Each representative is also provided with four garage spaces and two outside spaces for staff members; and each senator is assigned three inside spaces for senior staff aides, plus outdoor spaces as required. The General Services Administration (GSA) provides one parking space for senators in each home state office in a federally owned or leased building.

- Members may get their car **hand-washed** at the Capitol for a special $3 discounted rate. The average cost elsewhere in Washington is between $10 and $14.

- Members may **lease automobiles** on a long-term basis for carrying out their official duties. It should not surprise anyone that the lease terms are extraordinarily generous.

- Members have **free use of the House recording studio** to produce radio and TV spots for distribution as public-service announcements to commercial stations serving their home district. They also receive free satellite service for radio and TV transmissions.

- Speaking of communications, members are also entitled to **two WATS access phone lines** in their Washington residence. (Representatives who choose unlimited WATS lines receive half the long-distance allowance.) Each member may also access one Federal Telephone System (FTS) line for unlimited long-distance calling after business hours and on holidays and weekends.

- If the purpose of an event is to "discuss matters relating to official duties with a person other than members or staff," **any food or beverage expense** incurred by the member and his or her employees is reimbursable.

- **Flags** that have flown over the Capitol are available free to members to be given as gifts.

- All expenses, including framing, for **reproducing a member's photograph** for distribution to the media and constituents are reimbursable.

- Members receive **discounted** ($5, formerly free) **haircuts, manicures, shoeshines, and shoe repairs** at the Senate and House barber and beauty shops located in the Senate and House office buildings.

- Members and their families may **borrow materials for personal use** from the Library of Congress. Other United States citizens are forbidden to borrow these same materials.

- Members may request **special research projects** from the Library of Congress. The public may not.

- Members may **borrow framed reproductions of paintings and prints** from the National Gallery of Art for display in their office. The public? You guessed it!

- Members and their staff members may **shop at their own discount general store,** where taxpayer-subsidized merchandise is nominally priced. Both the Senate and the House recently decided to eliminate some fancy gift items, which instead will be sold with souvenirs in a gift shop open to the public. Just before this decision was made, staff aides anticipated such a move and literally stormed the store to buy expensive Mont Blanc pens, crystal candlesticks, and leather wallets at 5 percent above the store's wholesale cost. It is amazing that anything was left for the general public.

- Members, their staff members, and guests eat **subsidized meals** from congressional restaurants. Until October 1991, they were allowed to run a tab for their meals. That year some tabs exceeded $300,000 and in many cases were taking years to be paid (many members were never billed at all). Members now have a pay-as-you-eat plan. Another recent money-saving change will reduce the serving hours of the Senate restaurants from 8 A.M. to 3:30 P.M. The basement snack bar will have to suffice for evening dining.

- In the former House post office, State Department staff aides are available to members to expedite the

free processing of passport applications. Processing
for the general public, however, continues to take
the usual two weeks and cost $75.

• The Postal Service provides special handling of
"orange bag" franked mail that ensures members a
special **one-day delivery service.**

• Being catered to achieves its most conspicuous display when Capitol police regularly clear a path
through crowds as lawmakers stride down a hall. Special operator-assisted **"Members Only" elevators** are
reserved for their use. Guards also hold subway cars
for them, as they would do for any "King of the Hill."

• Ordinary citizens struggle each year with the intrica-
cies, obfuscations, and legalistic mumbo-jumbo of
their annual federal income-tax forms. And most
people generally pay dearly to have their tax returns
prepared by a tax professional. Members, on the
other hand, have a **special Capitol IRS office** to
assist in the preparation of their returns.

• Congress, on the off-chance that a war might be
fought within the United States proper, has con-
structed for itself a **top-secret bunker** capable of with-
standing the most powerful nuclear blast. It spends
many millions of dollars keeping this facility in a perfect state of readiness even today, after the dissolution of the Soviet Union has turned the specter of
nuclear warfare into the most remote possibility. It
goes without saying that in the event of a nuclear
attack, private citizens, even if they could find the
place, need not apply for admission. (And if I were a
member of the minority party, I wouldn't breathe
easy until I were safely inside.)

BANKING PRIVILEGES

Until October 1991, the House bank, run by the Sergeant At Arms, was used by all 440 members of the House of Representatives and its delegates. Much like commercial banks, the House bank (located on the first floor of the Capitol) took deposits, issued checkbooks and monthly statements, and cashed checks, both its own and those written on other banks. To conduct those transactions, it maintained an average daily balance of more than $1 million. Only House members were permitted to use these services. Unlike a commercial bank, the House bank provided free "overdraft" protection, honoring checks even if the account had insufficient funds.

In an age of automatic teller machines and computerized check clearing, the now-closed House bank was a financial anachronism relying on hand-written records, easy-going informality, and unquestioning service to its only account holders—members of Congress.

Operating since the early 1800s, none of the bank's rules was in writing and none of its staff, including the patronage-appointed House Sergeant At Arms, was a trained banker. The bank was not federally insured, paid no interest on checking accounts, and made no loans, but it is claimed that no taxpayer funds were involved in its operation. One can question, however, who paid the employee salaries and who bought its equipment (computers, for example).

SCANDAL IN THE HOUSE BANK

In the long and celebrated history of Congress, no tradition at the House bank is more firmly established than scandal.

In 1839, a cashier and his mistress, a local prostitute, made off with the House payroll ($75,000), never to be heard from again. Because deposit insurance was unheard of at the time, a wrenching debate ensued over whether the lost salaries should be reimbursed from the Treasury, which in today's currency would be more than $1 million. Rising to the occasion, Congress paid everyone back. Never let it be said that the members do not take care of their own.

In 1947, the House Sergeant At Arms was imprisoned for one year after trying to cover up a series of embezzlements from members' accounts' going back 20 years. Some of the proceeds had been used by a Florida congressman and his business partner to finance the congressman's campaigns and to speculate in losing real estate ventures. Swamplands, anyone?

Even after that scandal, abuses at the House bank were winked at with regularity. From 1832 to the present, leaders of the House have been regularly informed of overdrafts. None ever chose to end the practice, even after the House debated the propriety of the government's advancing pay to representatives without charging interest.

Audit reports prepared more than 30 years ago by the General Accounting Office (GAO) and made public during the current scandal show that one-third of the members' accounts had been overdrawn in the 1950s!

By 1972, the GAO found that 12,309 checks had been overdrawn; four years later, the number was 18,428. These overdrafts were referred to in the report, but mainly in pallid footnotes that all but obscured the depth of the problem.

What looked like a bank, called itself a bank, and in many respects acted like a bank was in reality a "cash club" in which House members could, and often did, write checks with impunity, regardless of whether they had enough funds to cover them.

More than two-thirds of House members regularly overdrew their accounts, and it has been reported that some were even cashing checks at the House post office, a practice forbidden by federal law.

A popular defense is that this bank wasn't really a bank, and that its record keeping was lackadaisical—haphazard at best. Certainly, it was a murky little financial institution, even by today's standards. However, what must be accepted is that this is exactly what the members wanted. For decades it existed just for the convenience of the House (whatever the Senate has is still a mystery), dispensing free checks and, in essence, free cash advances that often became free long-term loans. It wasn't a bank, though—it was a pot of gold.

True to form, House members could not practice restraint, and when 134 House members kited more than 8,300 checks in 1991, the lasagna hit the fan.

An Ethics Committee audit disclosed that during a 39-month period, 325 current and former House members had written more than 24,000 overdrafts at the now scandal-plagued House bank. They identified as "worst" offenders 22 members who wrote 11,424 overdrafts for more than $4.5 million.

According to the House Ethics Committee's dubious standards, the other 303 members were not labeled "abusers" because "an abuser is defined as one whose overdrafts exceeded their monthly pay at least nine times in the 39-month period examined." Thus if members exceeded their monthly income only eight times or spread out overdrafts over only 40 months, the Ethics Committee could not bring itself to label them as abusers. This is despite the fact that some deliberately overdrew their accounts to make interest-free loans to their own reelection campaigns. One irate House member publicly complained, "these people were getting very large interest-free loans . . . because they were members of Congress . . . They were doing something they knew was wrong."

Of potentially more serious consequence is the disclosure that some House members were improperly exchanging postage vouchers for cash. House records disclose that these members have engaged in extraordinary cash transactions totaling tens of thousands of dollars over the past five years.

These vouchers, which are essentially purchase orders drawn on the office accounts of members, are used to buy goods and services "for official purposes" from various congressional facilities. Knowingly converting these funds to personal use constitutes a criminal act more popularly known as "embezzlement."

These allegations have attracted the attention of the Justice Department, and federal prosecutors are investigating this matter.

CONCLUSION

Interestingly enough, members of Congress expected voters to understand because they assumed that everybody bounces checks. Actually, everybody doesn't. According to the American Bankers Association, only three-fourths of 1 percent of the more than 50 billion checks written yearly bounce. And a third of our banks don't even offer overdraft protection.

The problem is that members of Congress are detached from reality. They are so catered to, and so privileged, that none of the congressional conveniences (their banks, restaurants, post office, physicians, barber and beauty shops, etc.) treats them normally. This situation is simply business as usual. Members enjoy a particular entitlement and never question it. All of them assume that they are special people and that these special arrangements are their just due. They are, after all, **America's privileged class.**

2

Feathering Your Own Nest— How Sweet It Is!

During the Great Depression years, the United States Congress, in an attempt to display compassion by sharing the heavy burden and hard times all Americans were then experiencing, voted to reduce its own salary by one-half. This act, a tacit admission that Congress had failed in its responsibility to manage wisely, was a noble and laudable gesture.

That occasion is remarkable in that it marks the only instance in which Congress has ever denied itself for the benefit of its constituency. Never again has compassion been allowed to overcome greed.

CREATING YOUR OWN SALARY

With the power to raise its salary and benefits at will, Congress has seized every opportunity to increase its fortunes. These actions have only been mediated by the political climate of the times. Congress generally votes itself whatever amount it believes the voters will tolerate. As Congress increasingly has rigged the political process to ensure its continued incumbency, its actions have grown bolder. In 1990 and 1991, with a reelection rate of more than 98 percent in favor of the incumbency, members of Congress voted themselves 20 to 30 percent pay raises in the middle of the worst recession in modern U.S. history.

It's not the case that these pay raises are ever given a proper hearing or are publicly debated or treated like other bills involving the public tax dollar. Rather, like thieves in the night, members of Congress surreptitiously add pay-raise bills to essential and generally highly desirable bills as a last-second amendment, usually around midnight on the last day of the last session of the year.

These bills, which at best give the president a humongous political black eye and at worst shut down the federal government, are thus virtually veto-proof. Another common ploy is to include the pay raise as a (literally) last-minute amendment to a thousand-page omnibus bill in the hope that it will escape unnoticed in the crowd.

The House is usually the leader in these raids on the public treasury, followed shortly by the Senate's claim that parity must be the order of the day.

In defense of the Congress, at no time has it had the temerity to claim that these raises are based on merit. Its excuse is that members are only maintaining parity with the average private-sector, middle-class management employee. In making this claim, Congress totally disregards General Accounting Office (GAO) statistics that place congressional income in the upper 5 percent of the nation's wage earners and ignores the fact that private-industry management either run a successful profitable organization or get fired.

Legislation passed in 1990 gave senators a 9.9 percent pay boost (up to $98,360 annually) and raised House members' pay 7.9 percent (up to the same dollar amount). All members of Congress receive automatic annual cost-of-living raises (COLAs) of about 4 percent. However, in addition to these increases, House members voted themselves an additional 25 percent pay raise that began in 1991, bringing their annual salary to $129,500, which COLAs raised to $133,600 in 1993. (See fig. 2.1 on p. 24.)

In an attempt to justify this action, the House banned the acceptance of outside honoraria. Senators continued until 1991 to accept special-interest fees of up to 27 percent of their salaries for speeches or outside appearances before groups that lobby Congress. Then, chafing under what they considered a gross inequity and unable to resist temptation, the senators raised their own pay in a midnight session to approximate parity with the House. At least they also gave up their honoraria. It is signficant to note the underlying spending bill also liberalized rules that govern gifts received by lawmakers, and demands for a recorded vote were arrogantly swept aside.

House members may accept gifts of unlimited value from parties who have "no direct interest in legislation before Congress." Senators have a gift limit of $300 from any one source other than relatives. Gifts from interested sources are limited to $200 per year for House members and $100 per year for senators. Note that gifts under $75 do not have to be included in the aggregate total.

Lest you think all lawmakers are equal, think again. Lawmakers in leadership positions earn substantially more than do their colleagues. In 1992 the House Speaker earned $166,200 and House minority and majority leaders both received $143,800.

The Senate majority and minority leaders and the president pro tempore enjoy similar increased salary differentials.

United States congressional salaries are much greater than are those of political leaders in other western democracies. Members of the British Parliament operate on approximately 33 percent of the amount paid to members of the U.S. Congress, while Canadian Parliament members scrape by on only 50 percent of the U.S. salaries.

Ever mindful of the tax ramifications of these obscene salary increases, congressional staffers rose to the occasion, devising a bill that lowered the tax rate for the very bracket in which lawmakers had placed themselves! *Not only is Congress making more money than ever before, each Member will pick up a tidy extra $1,000 in new tax breaks!* At the same time, the average U.S. family is losing $1,440 in net worth to inflation and new taxes in the next year.

CREATING YOUR OWN RETIREMENT PLAN

Also, every time Congress raises its own salaries, it adjusts congressional pensions. This process happens automatically every year.

They even have what is considered to be one of the most generous group-retirement plans in existence. Members of Congress have left no stone unturned to ensure themselves a life of luxurious leisure after they leave the political arena.

Beginning in 1987, members have had the opportunity to invest as much as 10 percent of their base pay in a qualified 401(k) pension plan. At the time they passed this law, they limited investments by ordinary citizens to a maximum of 7 percent.

You should realize that taxpayers are also required to contribute to the congressional 401(k) benefit package. Taxpayers must match the first 5 percent of each member's salary investment, and potentially can pay as much as $6,200 for every participating member.

Members are also covered under the Social Security program. They have the additional option of participating in a high-octane version of the Civil Service Retirement System (CSRS) programs, in which 8 percent of their pay is deducted each year. According to government estimates, CSRS has an unfunded liability of more than $500 billion, which ultimately must come from taxpayers.

The National Taxpayers Union (NTU), a nonpartisan, nonprofit organization, has conducted an in-depth study of congressional pension programs. It has reached some astounding conclusions.

The NTU estimates that "almost half of all retired members of Congress living in May 1989 are projected to receive more than $1 million in lifetime Congressional pension benefits." (See appendix.)

The recent pay raises turn into golden parachutes for congressional incumbents, with 231 House members and 72 senators eligible to collect more than $1 million in lifetime benefits by 1993.

Benefits for retired legislators range from $609 a month for former representative Bella Abzug (D-NY) for her six years in Congress to $12,400 monthly—almost $150,000 a year—to former Senate majority leader Mike Mansfield for his more than 30 years of federal and military service.

By contrast, the typical retired federal civil servant gets a monthly pension of $1,297, and the average Social Security benefit for most retired Americans is $602 a month.

Thanks to cost-of-living adjustments (COLAs), some retired members' pensions are greater than their former House or Senate salaries.

These benefits are outrageously generous by any standard, with congressional pensions fully protected by the COLAs. Fewer than 10 percent of private-sector pensions offer formal COLAs. Congressional benefits are, in the majority of cases, two to three times larger than private-sector plans and are even more generous than pensions for federal workers. This list shows some of the reasons for this disparity:

1. The pension base is higher.
2. Members enjoy a much lower retirement age with full benefits.
3. Congressional benefit reduction for early retirement is only 1 to 2 percent as opposed to 4 percent for typical corporate benefits, with no Social Security benefits until age 62.

According to the *Senate Forums and Federal Pensions,* the lifetime pension benefits paid to the average career civil servant total $739,635 compared to $208,408 for the average private pension-plan participant.

Congressional retirement benefits are normally calculated by multiplying the number of years of federal service by 2.5 percent of the average of the three highest years' salaries. Depending on the number of years of service, members of Congress may begin drawing benefits as early as age 50.

David Keating of the National Taxpayers Union states, "Congress has protected itself from any economic harm that might result from its irresponsible spending policies . . . Few private-sector retirees have such protection from the ravages of inflation and recession . . . Many members of Congress could make more in retirement than a typical wage earner could earn in a lifetime . . . In future debates about the compensation of members of Congress, all factors, including the impact of pay increases on the pension liabilities of Congress, must be disclosed to the taxpaying public."

A Possible Solution from Our Forefathers

Strange as it may seem, our Founding Fathers were also quite concerned about the wisdom of permitting Congress to establish its own salary. At a time when members of Congress were paid $6 a day, or less than $1,000 a year, plus a stipend of $6 per mile for every mile traveled to attend sessions, James Madison introduced a congressional amendment to ban midterm salary increases.

"There is a seeming impropriety," Madison said, "in leaving any set of men without control to put their hand into the public coffers, to take out money to put in their pockets; there is a seeming indecorum in such power, which leads me to propose such a change."

Madison introduced his amendment more than 200 years ago. Politicians, true to their calling, were reluctant to ratify any amendment that limited their power to gouge the public. Only recently has Michigan become the 38th state to ratify this constitutional amendment. As public outrage grew over the latest congressional scandals, the speed of ratification increased, and since August 1992 the final state approvals necessary for ratification were accomplished.

The Madison amendment is simple. It says, "No law varying the compensation for the services of Senators and Representatives shall take effect, until an election of Representatives shall have intervened." Although this ammendment does not actually limit congressional salaries, it does bar Congress from raising the pay of members during their term in office and provides voters with an opportunity to express their approval or disapproval during the intervening election.

In today's world, this amendment poses some interesting legal questions. If it survives anticipated legal challenges from the state legislatures and is ultimately ratified by U.S. Archivist Don W. Wilson, will the yearly congressional cost-of-living adjustment (COLA) be forbidden?

COLAs are now added automatically to congressional pay based on changes in an employment cost index issued by the Labor Department. This index is the broadest gauge of pay raises for both blue- and white-collar workers. The congressional raises are one-half of a percentage point below that figure with a cap of 5 percent per year.

Although congressional leaders are publicly endorsing the spirit of the amendment, they are reported to be quietly working behind the scenes to seek ways to deny issuance of a certificate of ratification by the U.S Archivist. Amendment opponents have questioned its validity based on a 1921 Supreme Court ruling on the 18th amendment; in it, the court offered a nonbinding observation that ratification of the pay-raise amendment should have occurred soon enough to reflect the will of the people at the time.

In this context, the current Supreme Court should consider that public scorn for lawmakers who raise their own salaries has changed little during the intervening years and that public outrage about the inept performance of lawmakers now earning $133,600 annually (plus perks) is at an all-time high.

Note also that members of Congress who are or have been in prison continue to receive pensions for their federal service. Others with federal pensions (such as retired military personnel) who become convicted felons are subject to having their pensions forfeited.

CONGRESS'S GOLDEN NEST EGG

- The typical reelected incumbent will retire with an annual pension of $60,646 after 1995, and 26 lawmakers' annual pensions will exceed $89,500.
- The average lifetime benefit after 1995 is $1,917,432.
- If reelected in 1995, 18 House Members will boast lifetime pensions over $500,000; 186 will collect over $1,000,000; 68 will collect over $2,000,000; 23 are eligible for $3,000,000; and 3 are eligible for $4,000,000 in benefits.
- It has been estimated that the Golden Nest Egg pension perk as it is now structured could be worth another $60,000 in hidden annual income. Is it any wonder that the congressional barons have lost ' touch with the realities of retirement facing their constituencies?

The appendix of this book contains charts that list the potential retirement benefits for each member of Congress included in a study released by the National Taxpayers Union.

Congressional Pay Compared to Other American Workers

(Median Income) 1983-1993

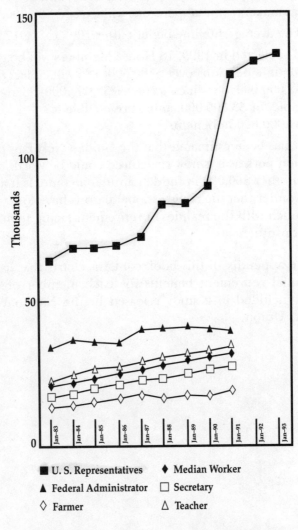

Legend:

■ U. S. Representatives   ◆ Median Worker

▲ Federal Administrator   □ Secretary

◇ Farmer   △ Teacher

Source: Bureau of the Census, Current Population Survey

Figure 2.1

3

Congressional Expense Allowances: the Ultimate Cheat Sheets

In the business world, expense accounts (sometimes referred to by insiders as the "cheat sheet") are a way of life. By and large, American businesspeople manage their company's affairs in large measure through the judicious expenditure of funds for the purpose of generating business.

Historically, expense-account allowances are the province of corporate marketing and sales departments, with the CEO as a notable exception. Expense budgets, especially travel and entertainment (T&E), are a major portion of their total operating budget. These departments are, after all, the firm's income and major profit generators; within reason, no price is too great to pay for their success.

Other departments make do with specific budgetary items for each public function in which they participate.

The generosity of these specific budgetary line items is in
direct proportion to the importance of the departmental
personnel involved.

However, those who live by the sword also die by the
sword: In bad times, overly generous budgets are often
the first items to come under the knife. Travel-and-enter-
tainment allowances are curtailed, sales reps book Motel
6 instead of the Hilton, and no one flies first-class. Meal
allowances are reduced, and if you must rent a car, it had
better be a compact model. Strict accountability is the
byword, and all expenditures must be justified in terms
of sales generated.

The business of government, however, marches to a
different drummer, at least as far as the congressional
operating budget is concerned. After all, when you have
voted for deficit spending, what else is there to do but
spend?

Each year, as part of the legislative budget, senators
and representatives are provided with expense allowances to cover costs associated with the fulfillment of
their official duties. These allowances vary depending on
such factors as the population of a senator's state or the
distance between a representative's home district and
Washington, D.C.

HOUSE EXPENSE ACCOUNTS

Each member of the House is entitled to the two following basic expense accounts.

- **The Clerk Hire Allowance** is used to hire staff for
  both the Washington and district offices. Each
  House member may hire up to 21 staff members;
  and in 1990, this allowance totaled $441,120 for each
  member of the House. In addition, each member is

allowed to hire one additional employee under the Lyndon B. Johnson Internship Program.

- **The Official Expenses Allowance** (OEA) is used to pay for expenses incurred in performing official duties. It is used in part to cover travel and telephone expenses between Washington and the member's home district and varies depending on the distance between the two. The OEA allowance is calculated according to the following criteria:

1. A base amount of $67,000
2. A minimum of $6,200 for travel, or an amount equivalent to the cost of 32 round-trips from Washington to the home district (based upon a formula that ranges from $0.23 to $0.39 per mile)
3. A minimum of $6,000 for long-distance telephone calls or an amount equivalent to the cost of 15,000 minutes of long-distance service based on daytime person-to-person rates
4. The cost of renting 2,500 square feet of office space in the member's district at the highest price charged by the General Accounting Office for federal office space.

Under the OEA criteria, the OEA varies from a low of $106,000 to a high of $302,218 per year. The average allowance is $146,388 for each year. In addition to the OEA, House members are given an additional $35,000 to purchase furnishings, carpets, draperies, and office equipment for district offices. Some of the items that can be charged to a member's OEA are as follows:

- **Office equipment,** including radios, typewriters, computers, televisions, copy machines, and video cassette recorders.
- **Stationery supplies** purchased from the House Office Supply Service. Supplies for personal use by

members and staff employees may also be bought by
paying a 10 percent surcharge.

- **Mobile homes** may be leased or rented for use as a
  mobile district office within the confines of the
  home district.

- **Education expenses** for courses of study and training
  programs, if approved by the Committee on Administration.

- **Plants, picture frames, and other display items** for
  the district office are given a special $250 per year
  allotment.

- **Books and newspapers** for office use.

- **Town-meeting advertisements and rent** for meeting
  halls.

- **Automobile rentals or leasing** on a long term basis.

- The ever popular **food-and-beverage expenses**
  incurred by a member or his or her employee during events whose purpose is to "discuss matters relating to official duties with a person other than the
  member's staff."

SENATE EXPENSE ACCOUNTS

The Senate does the House one better in that it provides
senators with not two but three expense accounts per
year. In addition, senators receive an allowance for office
space, furniture, and furnishings through the General
Services Administration (GSA). This allowance is based
on a $30,000 minimum for office space not in excess of
4,800 square feet. However, this can be increased by $734
for each authorized increase of 200 square feet.

The GSA is a one-stop shopping center for senators that provides all items of furniture and standard furnishings, including lamps, wastebaskets, floor mats, display racks, filing cabinets, and U.S flags for indoor display.

Additionally, the GSA supplies and maintains carpets and draperies, which are replaceable every seven years unless earlier replacement is authorized. (You know who does the authorization.)

The first budgetary item, the Administrative and Clerical Assistance Allowance (ACAA), varies according to the population of the senator's state. Senators from California, the most populous state, receive $1.7 million; but Wyoming senators for example, receive only $814,000. This allowance is used to hire as many employees as a senator needs.

The Legislative Assistance Allowance (LAA), the second budgetary item, is given to each senator to hire employees representing them on their committees. This allowance amounts to $269,000 per senator.

The third expense account, the Senatorial Official Office Expense Allowance (SOOEA), is determined by the distance between the senator's home state and Washington, D.C., as well as by the state's population. Thus a senator from Hawaii receives $156,000, while one from Delaware receives only $33,000.

The SOOEA pays for carrying out catch-all official duties items such as:

- For travel, senators are reimbursed for **actual transportation expenses for round-trip transportation** and are given a per diem of $126 per day (more for travel to Alaska and Hawaii). Additionally, they are reimbursed for any travel expenses essential to the transaction of official business.

- **Stationery and other office supplies** that can be purchased from commercial stores, GSA stores, or the Senate Stationery Room.

- **Communication expenses** such as telephone, telegrams, fax, or other phone services provided to the senator's office in Washington, D.C.

- **Mailing of official packages** through commercial carriers (or the postal service if not franked).

- **Subscriptions and clipping services** whether incurred in the home offices or in Washington, D.C.

Also, individuals selected by the senator to serve on panels or other bodies making recommendations for nominees to federal judgeships or service academies may be reimbursed for transportation, per diem, and certain other expenditures incurred in the performance of their official duties.

OFF-BUDGET SERVICES

In addition to the many benefits and services charged to members' expense allowances, they and their staffs are entitled to a host of other "off budget" services. The following services are in addition to benefits described elsewhere in this book.

Almost no member of Congress will deign to have his Washington office furnished in the austere government style so familiar to the average taxpayer. The excuse offered for the regally plush and sumptuous furnishings is that the good folks back home have a right to be impressed by their legislator's official place of business.

Thus, representatives request "special" (very expensive) furnishings from the Clerk of the House, and senators obtain their showcase furnishings from the Superintendent of Buildings, who acts as a representative for the Architect of the Capitol (who is responsible for the Capitol buildings and grounds).

Special furnishings obtainable from these Capitol purveyors include executive desks and plush swivel chairs, custom draperies, typing chairs, bookcases, leather couches and lounge chairs, table lamps, desks, coat trees, rugs, plush carpeting, made-to-order bookcases, glass tops for desks, refrigerators, smoking stands, filing cabinets, executive tables, conference tables, coffee tables, and customized venetian blinds.

Each Washington office receives a free *Webster's Unabridged Dictionary*. Plants are loaned by the U.S. Botanical Gardens, as are two framed reproductions from the National Gallery of Art. Maps are provided free by the Geological Survey.

Pictures, photos, and maps are framed free of charge by the Superintendent of Buildings' framing service.

GOING-AWAY GIFTS

Members leaving Congress may purchase (from one office only) their used furniture and furnishings at a depreciated value or fair market value, whichever is greater. (You really don't want to know how the fair market value is established.) The sumptuously furnished home offices of a great number of ex-members of Congress were obtained virtually by courtesy of the U.S. taxpayer.

You also should know about the special going-away gift the House of Representatives voted to give to retiring Speakers of the House. Always resentful of the exorbitant perks granted to outgoing presidents of the United States, the House quietly awarded outgoing Speakers the gift that keeps on giving: a plush, fully expensed office and staff, usually in a building with the member's name on it, ostensibly to enable him to wind down his political affairs without feeling any deprivation from leaving office.

Every Speaker since Carl Albert has enjoyed this lavish perk at a cost of millions to the taxpayer. Since Speaker Albert retired in 1977, his taxpayer-funded office expenses alone have exceeded $2.7 million. (How long does it take to wind down, anyway?)

These "retired" politicians continue to feed at the public trough long after their public service to the country has ceased. Instead, they service their own self-interest and incomes by brokering power, political favors, and insider contacts the same as any Washington lobbyist does. These generalists, however, serve no master but themselves and profit handsomely while the taxpayer continues to pay the bill. Who benefits from all of this? Certainly not the general public.

It is said that Washington is the world's greatest producer of paper. By this, I don't mean manufacturer of paper, I mean waster of paper. Tons and tons of the stuff are wasted. Enough to keep warehouse walls bulging ominously and shredders running 24 hours a day.

Each senator, for example, receives from the secretary of the Senate 1⅓ blank sheets of paper per adult constituent per year (no senator gets fewer than 1.8 million sheets per year). This amount is in addition to another huge amount of *free* letterhead sheets and envelopes provided each year; the envelopes are supplemented by rolls of continuous sheets for use with computer word-processor printers.

Paper used for town-meeting notices that announce only the time and place at which a senator will be available is also not charged to his paper allowance.

Paper has to be processed. If a senator determines that she is the recipient of an organized mail campaign and the senator's available office resources are insufficient, she may request the Sergeant At Arms to handle the mail. All expenses for this service are paid by the Sergeant At Arms, including the paper used for responses.

The general office equipment used in Senate offices, including the home offices, is supplied and maintained by the Sergeant At Arms. Items in this category include signature-signing machines, letter folders, letter inserter and sealers, paper cutters with stands, electric or manual typwriters, calculators, copyholders, noise suppressors, electric pencil sharpeners and staplers, recorders and transcribers, telephone answering machines, and time recorders.

In the fiscal year 1990, the legislative branch budget totaled nearly $2 billion and was expected to increase by half a billion in 1991. Thus taxpayers that year spent an average of more than $3½ million per lawmaker, including congressional salaries and support services, to fund the legislative branch of government.

The support structure provided by taxpayers to each member of Congress clearly demonstrates that their numerous privileges, perks, and allowances do more than merely facilitate the office duties of legislators and their staffs. Legislators are in fact pampered, sustained, and nourished in a sumptuous and virtually imperial atmosphere as foreign to the private sector as are the regal trappings of royalty to a democracy—unless, of course, you are a member of **America's privileged class.**

4

Congressional Exemptions and the Ethical Consequence

———

It would seem that the leaders of a democratic republic would require all avenues of exchange and communication between themselves and their constituency to remain open. They seemingly would avail themselves of every opportunity to share in the common social order to better evaluate the impact of their leadership. It is a given that these leaders would insist on full participation in the legal and social structure they had crafted to determine its equity, effectiveness, and acceptance among the people they represent.

Only a privileged class insists on exempting itself from many of the important laws it has imposed on its own electorate. Only a privileged class would consider many of its own statutes too onerous and intrusive to be endured by themselves. Only a privileged class considers its status to be so apart, so superior, to its constituency.

The Congress of the United States is this type of privileged class.

Since 1933, Congress has systematically exempted itself from any law that might require it to admit or accept any form of regulatory oversight by any other government agency. Among the three constitutionally recognized equal branches of the United States government, only Congress has embarked on a program of setting itself apart as the superior branch—the privileged class.

EXEMPTIONS FROM IMPORTANT LAWS

This section lists some of the laws from which Congress has exempted itself. They are numerous, and their impact on our society is profound.

- **The Social Security Act of 1933** imposes payroll taxes on most of the U.S. work force for retirement benefits. Congress has feathered its own nest with one of the world's most generous retirement programs, but not until the 1980s did public pressure force members to pay Social Security taxes and share financial responsibility for entitlement programs run amok under congressional mismanagement. Congress did not dispense with its other retirement program, however.

- **The National Labor Relations Act of 1935** gives employees the right to organize in labor unions and engage in collective bargaining with employers. However, no one forces Congress to the bargaining table, no matter how justifiable the issue may be.

- **The Minimum Wage Act of 1963** sets wage and overtime standards. Congress rarely pays its general employees the minimum wage, even though it requires every other employer in the United States to do so.

- **The Equal Pay Act of 1963** requires that men and
  women receive the same pay for doing the same
  jobs. This act speaks for itself. (Pity the poor female
  congressional staffer who expects the same salary as
  her male counterpart.)
- **The Civil Rights Act of 1964** bars discrimination in
  the workplace and across American society. Until the
  Anita Hill hearings, the average American taxpayer
  did not realize that female congressional employees
  were not protected from sexual discrimination, even
  though many such charges had been raised and were
  subsequently generally ignored.
- **The Freedom of Information Act of 1966** forces public disclosure of public documents. You can get your
  records from the FBI, the CIA, and even the IRS.
  Information about or from inside the Congress?
  Good luck!
- **The Age Discrimination Act of 1967** bars discrimination based on age in employment and promotion
  and protects workers from forced retirement. Anything that might interfere with the congressional
  patronage system is simply not tolerated.
- **The Occupational Safety and Health Act of 1970** sets
  health and safety standards for the workplace—every
  workplace in the country except for Congress.
- **The Equal Employment Opportunity Act of 1970** provides for equal employment opportunity regardless
  of age, color, sex, or ethnic origin. The opportunity
  is equal everywhere except where patronage reigns
  supreme.
- **The Title IX of the Higher Education Act of 1972**
  provides for, among other things, equal disbursement of funds without regard to gender within similar school departments in educational institutions
  that receive government funds. A girls' basketball

team for example, is supposed to have a budget
equal to the budget for the boys' team. Congress,
however, disburses without regard to gender rights.

- **The Rehabilitation Act of 1973** expands the rights of
the disabled. However, this law is superseded by
1990's **Americans with Disabilities Act,** under which
complainants may take a grievance to the Senate Ethics Committee but may not sue, as they are entitled
to do against a private employer.

- **The Privacy Act of 1974** bars the government from
disclosing personal information about an individual
without his or her permission. The congressional
exemption protects members from slander and libel
suits and the legal responsibility to ensure the truth
and accuracy of their public statements. On the Senate or House floor, members can disclose anything,
and they can say anything they want with absolute
impunity.

- **The Age Discrimination Act Amendments of 1975** in
part raised the mandatory retirement age of government employees from 65 to 70. Considering the number of congressional septuagenarians, when you get
a good thing going, hang in there.

- **The Ethics in Government Act of 1978** set up the
independent counsel system to investigate allegations of executive-branch misdeeds. Congress natu-
rally is above investigation. (Whoever heard of a
congressional misdeed?)

This law was designed to permit Congress to
harass the executive branch while ostensibly keeping
itself at arm's length. At taxpayers' expense, the
members of Congress hire an independent counsel,
or IC (correction—a special prosecutor), to pursue
alleged infractions of congressional edicts without
getting their own hands dirty. The last IC of note is

Lawrence Walsh, of Irangate notoriety, whose record to date consists of one minor conviction on a plea bargain. Everything else has been overturned, or is expected to be overturned, on appeal. The cost to taxpayers now exceeds $100 million. Fury hath no equal like a congressperson scorned.

- **The Conflict of Interest Laws** bar other government officials from dealing with matters in which they may have a financial interest. These laws also specifically prohibit executive-branch types from dealing with others about government matters for a two-year period after leaving government service. However, your everyday congressperson can still turn up as your friendly lobbyist the day after he leaves Congress.

- **The Sunshine Act** requires government agencies to conduct their business in public. It seems reasonable, but not to Congress.

- **The Inspector General Act** requires the president to appoint inspectors general to combat fraud and abuse within the executive branch. However, investigating Congress is a major taboo, no matter how much fraud and abuse are evident.

- **The Civil Rights Restoration Act of 1988** says that victims of intentional discrimination or harassment based on sex, religion, or disability may seek punitive and compensatory damages with financial caps based on a firm's work-force number. The burden of proof falls on employers to demonstrate that any employment practice with a discriminatory effect is job-related for the position in question and constitutes a business necessity. Congressional employees are not covered by Title VII protections. Because of extreme public pressure (the Anita Hill case again), protections were extended to employees of both the

Senate and House of Representatives. However, *each body independently defines it own rules for dealing with discrimination claims.*

DISCIPLINARY EFFORTS AND ETHICS REVIEWS

True to form, Congress does not permit any other government body to investigate, judge, or punish its members. It reserves this power strictly for itself and bases this position on the Constitution's "equal but separate" clause. Because Congress makes the laws, it can define itself according to the laws it passes. Other branches of government without legislative power are denied the opportunity to define their powers in this way and are left at the mercy of the Congress in this respect.

However, Congress, like any other public institution, must ultimately respond to public opinion. Thus it was finally forced to develop a mechanism whereby the public felt that some checks and balances were placed on congressional shenanigans. Enter the ethics committees, the congressional answer to how to slap yourself on the wrist painlessly.

No matter—the latest scandal to unleash a feeding frenzy on Capitol Hill demonstrated again that Congress has saddled itself with an unworkable ethics review process. The public perception is that collegiality outranks fairness and that investigations take far too long and usually come to conclusions that satisfy no one. The public also believes that serious allegations are normally superficially reviewed by the ethics panel, and that—unless public and media pressure is relentlessly brought to bear—these allegations are quietly disposed of in some smoke-filled back room.

Judging the conduct of its members is problematic for any organization. In an egalitarian body like Congress, where personal influence is the operative mechanism, it is exceedingly difficult to judge friends, party colleagues, and powerful political cronies with decades worth of political IOUs at their disposal.

Any ethics investigation that concludes with a minor slap on the wrist or with the charges dropped completely is sure to be analyzed, by the media and such powerful private groups as Congress Watch and Common Cause, in terms of power and influence rather than on the merits of the case.

Within these watchdog groups, where there is smoke, there is fire. No censure or reprimand is strong enough. They view each vindication as a whitewash that highlights the pervasive and increasing corruption in government. By this yardstick, no member ever is punished sufficiently, nor is he ever justifiably innocent.

In reality, the House and Senate have tried to structure the ethics review process as fairly as possible (that is, as fairly as the membership will permit itself to be judged). The two ethics committees are the only truly bipartisan panels in Congress with equal numbers of Democrats and Republicans represented. Inexplicably, these committees do not employ the services of either House or Senate counsel but rather retain outsiders who cannot be held accountable for their performance. Despite the best efforts to achieve fairness, the public perception of their activities is that the whole system is a sham.

What the public fails to appreciate is that it is not actual lawbreaking at issue here but rather congressional rules (nebulous rules to be sure, but rules nonetheless). Thus reasonable solutions are not readily available to those who seek justice in the conventional sense, and Congress absolutely will not impose sanctions on any but the most egregious offenders of its own overly generous, self-protective rules of conduct.

The reluctance of the members to restructure congressional rules by formalizing them into specific rather than generalized codes is understandable considering their freewheeling history of largely unfettered conduct. Yet that is what must happen if Congress is to survive as a meaningful, constructive organization. In its present form, Congress is unworkable, unproductive, unmanageable, and unstable. Unless it becomes truly accountable for its activities and the actions of its membership, both individually and collectively, it will be disgraced beyond redemption.

MOVING TOWARD ACCOUNTABLITY

Reformation of the ethics review process is an absolute first priority if the legislators and the public are to concentrate their energies and interests on the nation's real problems.

If Congress truly wants accountability, it would be wise to adhere to the principle set forth by James Madison in Federalist Paper Number 57: "Members of Congress can make no law which will not have its full operation on themselves and their friends, as well as on the great mass of society. This has always been deemed one of the strongest bonds by which human policy can connect the rulers and the people together."

Until this accountability is accomplished and legislative ethics are no longer paper tigers, the American people will continue to consider Congress a mockery and view it with the contempt it so richly deserves.

5

"Air USA"—the Only Way to Fly

One of Washington's best-kept secrets is that one of the world's plushest airlines is government-owned. Referred to in some quarters as Air USA or Air Congress, its primary function is to chauffeur members of Congress and top administration officials anywhere their hearts desire. Although the airline is maintained, operated, and financed by your tax dollars, ordinary taxpayers are not allowed to use it, except under rare, special circumstances.

THE GOVERNMENT'S AIRLINE

The flagship is the 89th Air Wing's Air Force One. Along with its sister ship, Air Force Two, this fleet of 26 military winged aircraft and 19 helicopters is provided for the use of top White House officials, cabinet officers, and members of Congress on a no-questions-asked basis more than 900 times a year. The annual cost to taxpayers is $150

million, according to the General Accounting Office
(GAO).

A great favorite with members of Congress, these
flights are especially popular with large delegations
engaging in overseas junketing.

The GAO's study of the use of the 89th Air Wing
showed that no attempt is made to determine whether
the trips are justified or whether less costly commercial
flights are available.

In addition to the costs associated with the flights
themselves, the 89th Special Air Mission, stationed at
Andrews Air Force Base, carries a hefty maintenance and
operating budget of more than $10 million per year.

The GAO report confirmed that in the majority of
cases, the use of 89th Air Wing aircraft was considerably
more expensive than the use of commercial aircraft for
similar trips. At times, the cost is ten times greater in
taking a military jet than it would be for flying a dozen
people from Washington to Los Angeles on commercial
flights. Besides the cost of fuel for the planes, taxpayers
pay for a 1,600-person crew of military and civilian
employees who maintain and repair the VIP aircraft.

The GAO concluded that the rules for traveling on the
VIP flights are so broad and vague that they are virtually
meaningless. It recommended that such flights be made
only in exceptional cases and with each justification fully
documented.

These VIP aircraft are not the bucket-seat, sparsely con-
figured planes normally seen in military action films.
They easily rival accommodations found in luxury private
jets. Their interiors have been painstakingly designed
with plush carpeting and richly upholstered sleeper-style
seats, and they are sumptuously furnished with every conceivable amenity, including well-stocked bars and gour-
met pantries. The service provided by well-trained military personnel (these highly prized assignments are very

motivational) is invariably impeccable, and the pilots are among the best the Air Force has to offer.

According to Defense Department figures, Air Force One, a Boeing 747 jumbo jet, costs about $25,000 an hour to fly. This figure is calculated by dividing the funds budgeted for the aircraft's annual operation by its antici-pated flying hours. However, the hourly cost of presiden-tial travel, for example, is considerably higher than $25,000 because a similar backup plane is usually flown to an airfield near the facility used by the president, and at least one cargo plane carries vehicles for the presiden-tial motorcade.

Additionally, dozens of support staff, including Secret Service agents, communications officials, and White House staff members, make advance preparation visits and incur transportation, hotel, and meal costs that are paid for by the government.

By one estimate, including the cost of flying advance teams to make arrangements, the cost for air travel alone for former President Bush's trip to Japan in 1992 exceeded $1.4 million.

None of these costs exists as a budgetary line item. Costs associated with presidential domestic travel are placed in the Pentagon budget, and the State Depart-ment covers most costs associated with presidential over-seas missions.

JUSTIFYING THE COST OF AIR TRAVEL

Everyone agrees that the president of the United States should be provided with appropriate transportation for official occasions. And no one would argue with the sec-retary of state and the secretary of defense's being given appropriate air transportation for their many foreign missions. No one questions the necessity for these government planes because of the obvious need for security and secure communications requirements at all times. And, in all fairness, *appropriate* should also mean *comfortable,* well-furnished accommodations that contain amenities essential to providing the occupants with a safe, restful journey. However, should it be the taxpayers' responsibility to provide similar travel accommodations for their personal or political journeys within the U.S.?

PERSONAL AIR TRAVEL IN THE CABINET

Consider some of the personal travel by members of the administration. Everyone is, or should be, familiar with the travels of former presidential Chief of Staff John Sununu. He eschewed commercial airlines with a passion, jokingly labeling his travels as Air Sununu and comparing his flight frequency to that of the United Nations' air strikes during the Desert Storm operation. It was all right for him to joke because he didn't have to pay the airfare. Of course, somebody did . . .

Also, don't you wonder why taxpayers were saddled with the expense of former Secretary of State Baker's travel to visit his home state of Texas or his ranch in Wyoming? The *Milwaukee Journal,* citing an unreleased draft audit prepared by the GAO, reported that 11 such trips over two years cost taxpayers $371,599.

The secretary claimed that he made full reimbursement with respect to any personal travel. What he didn't say was that government policy required him to reimburse only on the basis of commercial coach fare (government employees are only entitled to fly coach), plus $1; thus Baker's travel on military jets cost many times the amount he paid. In this case, the 11 trips cost taxpayers a total of $388,758, and reimbursements totaled only

$17,159. (He claims that his records show reimbursements of $38,453, still only 10 percent of the original cost.) Considering the present state of the economy, it is reasonable to assume that this money could have been put to far better use than stroking the ego of the secretary of state.

Baker, after being shown these figures in a draft audit by the GAO (and being always a prudent politician), immediately began using commercial airlines for his personal travel within the United States. On commercial flights, the secretary was accompanied by his usual bodyguards and was given a secure cellular telephone. Don't delude yourself into believing that the funds for these flights came out of the secretary's pocket.

Baker's open-mindedness prompted the chairman of the Senate Federal Services subcommittee to call on other executive branch officials to do the same and said of the secretary: "It sounds like he's saying, 'I didn't do anything wrong and I promise not to do it again.' But the bottom line is, his change of policy is going to save the taxpayers money, and I'm glad he has reconsidered."

It would not be fair to close this commentary about the great frequent fliers on Air USA without mentioning the greatest of them all—Samuel Skinner, former President Bush's chief of staff. Skinner picked up the travel banner from his predecessor, Sununu, without missing a takeoff. Skinner came to his office from his previous post as secretary of transportation with an imposing record of using government jets to go absolutely anywhere, at any time, for any reason—especially for golf (a game he loved to play with his good buddy, former Vice President Dan Quayle, another seasoned frequent flier).

A flying buff, Skinner even used his previous office to upgrade his personal flying skills to include multijet aircraft. Without permission, he spent more than $60,000 in lessons and simulator time, all charged to the American taxpayer. Skinner's stated justification was that, as secretary of transportation, he needed frequent, hands-on-the-controls access to the friendly skies to evaluate transportation conditions properly.

Apparently, Skinner considered travel and transportation as one-dimensional because no one could recall having seen him recently on a train, boat, or bus. Perhaps we should all be thankful for that because heaven only knows what it might have cost us to qualify him as a ship's master or locomotive engineer.

In an incredible exposé on CBS's "60 Minutes," a cost analysis comparing Skinner's use of government aircraft to commercial airlines placed his abuse of privilege so far beyond the pale that it would make even Sununu blush (especially after an equally thorough itinerary investigation disclosed that virtually every trip included a golf game or other personal function).

In case you wondered, Skinner acquired his taste for feeding at the taxpayer travel trough while serving as a public prosecutor.

CONGRESS AND COMMERCIAL AIR TRAVEL

Members of Congress have been particularly resourceful when it comes to securing special privileges in the commercial travel arena. Each member and their employees are reimbursed for all expenses incurred while traveling on official business. The definition of "official" is usually left up to the member. This reimbursement includes meals, lodging, and transportation in commercial carriers and in private or leased vehicles. In this regard, members and their employees are also allowed to take advantage of special discounts on travel offered by the airlines, hotels, and motels.

Additionally, House members are free to convert frequent-flier mileage awards from taxpayer-paid trips for all personal travel, whether it's back to the district or to an island retreat. The Senate takes a firmer stand, regarding frequent-flier awards as Senate property not convertable to personal use except for "separating" members, who can purchase the mileage at the going government rate. The vast majority of government critics say that membership in the mileage clubs is a clear conflict of interest, particularly for members who ponder airline-industry issues.

Other government employees are not permitted to take personal trips with the bonus miles because legal rulings (from which Congress exempts itself) have declared them to be government property.

To ensure minimum inconvenience, members may use the congressional travel service and purchase airline tickets at a special ticketing office located in the Longworth House office building. Members of Congress get free upgrades to first class on their airline travels, and anyone traveling more than twice a year (this probably excludes only congressional pages) receives a Diner's Club U.S. government charge card to pay authorized travel expenses.

Speaking of authorization, it is important to appreciate that Senate leaders, the Speaker of the House, or committee Chairs must authorize all foreign trips by members of Congress and their employees. Members may travel to foreign countries on authorized congressional business or by executive request or appointment. In this regard, the House committee system has spawned so many subcommittees that almost any third-term member can be called "Mr. Chairman" and enjoy additional staff and such perks as being able to approve foreign travel.

According to reports filed by congressional committees and officials, member and staff foreign travel cost $13.5 million during the 100th Congress (1987–88). Funds for foreign travel by members of Congress are appropriated as part of the State Department's budget and financed by taxpayers. Based on current expense estimates, it is a safe assumption that virtually no request for authorization is denied.

MILITARY AND FOREIGN FREEBIES

Members and their families can use military officers' quarters, clubs, recreational facilities, base exchanges, and commissaries at military installations throughout the world. The free recreational privileges include golf, tennis, hunting, and fishing. They are also greeted with open arms at all U.S. embassies and official residences. After all, they are traveling on the State Department's budget, for which they control the allocation and approval of funds.

Members of Congress and their spouses and dependents may accept travel-related gifts within foreign countries offered by foreign governments or other foreign entities (like an Arab sheik) when the travel relates to official duties of the member. These gifts of travel may include food, beverages, lodging, transportation, and entertainment.

CAMPING CLOSER TO HOME

For those who prefer the more natural outdoor surroundings of the United States, the Department of Interior accommodates members and their families at national parks for below-normal rates and sometimes in special housing not available to the general public. (This last perk has undergone some adjustments, however.)

Get elected to Congress and see the world. As Robin Leach would put it, experience your own "champagne wishes and caviar dreams," courtesy of the American taxpayer.

6

World Travel à la Mode, Courtesy of U.S. Taxpayers

A *junket,* according to Webster's, is "a trip made ostensibly for official business, enjoyed at public expense." In other words, it's a pleasure excursion.

Because a congressional junket is perhaps the most easily recognizable abuse of the public treasury (what other taxpayer rip-off has its own dictionary definition?), it seems only fair to devote a full chapter to this fascinating subject, even though many of the perks and privileges that make congressional junketing such a popular pastime have already been disclosed.

A former member of Congress recalled that, shortly after he was first elected, he was taken aside by a colleague who offered to "show him the ropes." "He quite blatantly told me the best part of the job was that you could travel anywhere in the world in royal style, your wishes attended to by the U.S. Embassy staffers." That comment did not cover the half of it. As he later learned,

"extravagantly opulent" is the congressional way of life—
it's the only way to travel.

When most U.S. officials travel abroad on government
business (as they put it), they stay in a class of hotels
most American taxpayers couldn't afford on a dream
vacation. However, the U.S. taxpayer foots the bill so that
the "public servant" can travel in style. Somehow, this
does not seem to be the way the system is supposed to
work.

BASING TRAVEL RATES ON LUXURY STANDARDS

When the pencil pushers and their staff members travel
to Tokyo, for example, they stay at the Hotel Okura,
recently ranked as the fourth best hotel in the world.
Located next door to the U.S. Embassy, the Hotel Okura
(with its seven restaurants, fitness center, in-room massages, shopping mall, and business service center with
multilingual secretaries and modern electronic communications facilities) is not the place where just members
of Congress, diplomats, and White House staffers rest
their bones. The U.S. Embassy also routinely books
planeloads of low-level bureaucrats into its marbled halls
and plush accommodations.

We don't expect our public servants to double-bunk at
the Motel 6 (although, considering the national debt,
perhaps we should), but we do expect them to follow the
federal standard and stay in "adequate, suitable, and
moderately priced" hotels. If that is the standard, how do
they get away with staying in such luxury digs? Until federal auditors wised up, taxpayers were paying $160 per
night per room, another $64 for meals, and $23 a day
walking-around money. Pretty spiffy, eh?

The State Department inspector general's auditors surveyed travel records from around the world and found that daily travel allowances were often based on the rates of the ritziest hotels and world-class restaurants. Smart travelers simply took the per diem based on the high-priced facilities, stayed in cheaper accommodations, and then pocketed the difference—all perfectly legal.

In London, government travelers reported using the elegant Grosvenor House overlooking Hyde Park the most, at $180 per night. However, the embassy's visitors' log disclosed that fewer than 3 percent of the guests actually stayed there. Instead, most were at the Mandeville Hotel, which cost less than half as much.

Likewise, in Paris, while being paid lodging rates based on the Intercontinental, most lodgers bunked at the Pullman, again at almost half the price.

When you consider that the federal overseas travel budget exceeds $300 million a year (not including airfare) and that the auditors examined per diem rates in 48 cities and 60,000 official visits, it is easy to see how the U.S. government squanders millions of dollars on travel each year.

Why hasn't this waste been stopped? There are two major reasons. First, much of this travel is done by members of Congress and their staffers, and we know that their greed has no limits. Second, embassy officials deliberately distorted hotel and restaurant prices to boost per diems. Why? Because the per diems are the basis for their own living allowances. What a system!

ACCEPTING TRAVEL PERKS FROM OUTSIDERS

It should come as no surprise that many of the trips taken by members of Congress are not paid for directly by the taxpayer. Despite intensive public attention over congressional ethics violations, most lawmakers have not cut back on accepting free travel from companies and special-interest groups. These trips are not merely accepted—quite the contrary—they are blatantly solicited.

Many lawmakers contend that these trips are no vacation but are necessary for them to reach out to parties with interests before the Congress. In addition to benefiting the interest groups, these trips enable members to befriend lobbyists and others who can be important adjuncts to their campaign fund-raising. Also, they often provide a chance for a free trip to their home state in luxurious corporate aircraft.

Senators accepted 506 expense-paid trips in 1989 from corporate or trade groups, compared to 452 in 1988 and 669 in 1987. Although many of these trips were in connection with speaking appearances before particular groups, in numerous cases organizations paid for trips for senators who also sat on committees with jurisdiction over their industries.

A prime example of this flagrant flaunting of the conflict-of-interest provisions of Senate ethics rules is provided by Senator Dave Durenburger (R-MN), who led his colleagues with 20 trips, of which 10 were paid for by health-related groups. It should come as no surprise to learn that Durenburger sits on subcommittees of the Senate Finance Committee that have jurisdiction over health issues.

Other frequent free travelers are Senators Hatch (R-UT) and Jeffords (R-VT) with 14 trips each. Senators Conrad (D-ND) and Robb (D-VA) are close on their heels with 13 free rides apiece.

Joan Claybrook, the president of Public Citizen, a Ralph Nader-founded research organization, says that expense-paid trips should be prohibited. She asserts that "these groups are willing to pick up the junket tabs because it provides them with a unique opportunity to gain access to lawmakers."

Public Citizen recommends that the government reimburse members who take such trips at the standard travel rates that apply to all federal employees.

Beginning in 1990, Senators are not allowed to accept gifts of travel that exceed three days for domestic trips and seven days for trips outside the U.S., excluding travel time. The change, a part of the Ethics Reform Act of 1989, places no restrictions on the amount any group can provide for such a trip.

The House ethics manual says that industry may pay for trips that make staff members "better informed regarding subject matter closely related to their official duties." Uh-huh.

Thus as action on clean-air legislation loomed close by in 1991, industries with large stakes in this legislation flew staff members of influential committees around the country on what were euphemistically called education tours. In this context, 18 aides on a natural-gas industry tour spent two nights at Walt Disney World's Resort Hotel in Orlando, and 5 staff members on a two-day Union Carbide tour spent the night in New Orleans' French Quarter.

Other trips have been sponsored by the Aerospace Industries Association, the Motor Vehicles Manufacturers Association, and the American Gas Association together with the Interstate Natural Gas Association of America. We can only hope that their itinerary was more appropriate to their legislative responsibilities.

WHEN IS A JUNKET A JUNKET?

If it looks like a junket and behaves like a junket, is it a junket? If it is taken by people who consider themselves too important to fly on commercial airlines and too privileged to pay for any recreational pleasure out of their own pocket while stealing time from the taxpayers, it's a junket!

Consider a congressional delegation of the House Select Committee on Narcotics Abuse and Control whose members all decided to learn about drug trafficking on a recent trip to Korea, Hong Kong, Laos, Thailand, and Hawaii—the very best of the Sun Belt and the Shopping Belt. This committee, led by Representatives Rangel (D-NY) and Coughlin (R-PA), requested that the Air Force provide a plane large enough for them to take their spouses (and ostensibly also to hold all the shopping goods they planned to bring home). The 89th Special Air Wing (good old Air USA) obliged with a C-135, the military version of a Boeing 707, which seats 60 people; then the committee, all six members and five wives, happily took off to all points east at a cost to taxpayers of $138,195.50. If the committee had been satisfied with a less prestigious aircraft (a 16-passenger Air Force Gulfstream, for example) it could have saved taxpayers $32,357.25, and saved even more by flying first-class on a commercial jetliner.

Lest you think that this type of junket is highly unusual, consider a recent trip to Europe by Senator Mark Hatfield (D-OR), his wife, and three aides. They flew to Brussels on this selfsame 60-passenger C-135 and, after picking up Senator Lugar (R-IN) and his wife, left for a 12-day fact-finding trip about human rights in Bulgaria, Rumania, and Czechoslovakia. This trip cost the taxpayers $111,609. Of course, if they had flown first class on a commercial airliner, all seven would have spent only $31,479.

In all fairness, on some occasions the use of military aircraft is justified, generally for security purposes and sometimes even to save money. For example, the prestigious Paris Air Show, an annual international extrava-

ganza, attracts politicians like honey attracts a bear. Four
Air Force planes loaded with members of Congress, their
spouses, staffers, and friends attended this soiree, with
the airfare costing U.S. taxpayers about $221,800. No
estimate is available for the ground expenses totaling
many thousands of dollars more than the air-travel costs.
However, the Air Force travel orders authorizing the use
of the aircraft noted that passengers were eligible to use
"post exchange, commissary, mess and other facilities
incident to this travel on the same basis as do officers of
the services."

Some may quibble about the necessity of four delegations totaling 101 people and perhaps may even question
the necessity for attending at all. However, anything
billed as the "quintessential place for the latest technol-
ogy that's in the sky" carries sufficient justification to
attract a congressperson. I mean, like here is a bona fide
reason for this junket, and they can't help if it's in Paris.

However, back to costs. The Air Force estimated that
the operational cost of the largest aircraft was about
$89,879; the smaller two cost $47,702 each, and the
smallest cost $36,533—a total of $221,800. By compari-
son, if the congressional delegation, staffers, and guests
had traveled on commercial business-class, the cost would
have been $150,000. First-class tickets, the way members
of Congress prefer to fly, would have cost nearly twice as
much. Tourist-class, of course, costs about 20 percent less
than business-class fares, but that would have been too
tacky for members of Congress and not nearly as much
fun.

This junket was all aboveboard and completely in line
with government regulations insofar as spouses, staffers,
and friends were concerned. (It says a lot for the regulations, doesn't it?)

Why expect a member of Congress to bother with commercial airliners when a private jet is so much more con-

venient and prestigious? Why expect junketing lawmakers to save money and fly in commercial airliners with
the ordinary folks who put them in their lofty office?
Why not, indeed? The abuse of privilege by the congressional nouveau royalty has placed them beyond any rational defense. Even on those rare occasions when congressional types pack a schedule so full of business or travel
to an area so remote that military aircraft are justified, it
has been demonstrated repeatedly that the cost-benefit
ratio is so disproportionately bad as to warrant cancella-
tion. (This will never happen.)

CROSSING THE LEGAL LINE

Consider a March 1991 trip by 12 members of Congress
who visited Kuwait. Their expenses were paid for by the
Fluor Corporation, at Kuwait's request, over the strong
objections of the Speaker of the House, Thomas Foley.

Even after the House Ethics Committee told the congress members that they could not accept a trip paid for
by a foreign government, and after Foley expressed his
strong concerns that U.S. corporate sponsoring might
not justify the trip (stating that it would be at best a
superficial cover for a trip improperly financed by
Kuwait), the group members told Foley that they were
going anyway and promptly proceeded to do so.

This four-day visit seemed to be Kuwait's way of saying
thanks to its major supporters in Congress and to others
who assisted in rebuilding the war-torn country. Others
on the trip were senior American business executives and
prominent defenders of Kuwait's cause. Secretary of
Commerce Robert Mosbacher went along to represent
the Bush administration. It is estimated that expenses for
the 12 congress members cost Fluor about $60,000. All
this happened despite congressional rules that bar travel

from the United States to a foreign country under the sponsorship of a foreign government.

Will Congress huff and puff in indignation? Not for very long, if at all. The congressional hypocrites will not go so far as to have the kettle call the pot black.

So you see, a junket doesn't have to be legal, it doesn't have to be according to the rules, it doesn't have to be approved, and it most certainly doesn't have to benefit taxpayers or be of any legitimate value to the United States government. A junket only has to be fun, and—of course—be limited to the privileged class.

7

Washington, D.C., the Congressional Camelot

"The Congress shall have the power . . . to exercise exclusive legislation in all cases whatsoever over such district (not exceeding 10 miles square) as may by the cession of particular States and the acceptance of Congress, become the seat of government of the United States."

The United States Constitution

Throughout its history, the District of Columbia's government has been changed, studied, supported, criticized, financed, debated, expanded, and reorganized, all under the control of the United States Congress.

LESS THAN A DEMOCRACY

Viewed by most United States citizens as a city that belongs to all the people of the nation, not just to the residents of Washington, the District is treated by Congress as its personal fiefdom—a congressional Camelot over which it exerts absolute financial and legal jurisdiction and exercises its responsibilities and privileges with autocratic deliberation.

The history of Washington, D.C., as the capital of the United States makes the city a preeminent center of world politics and, therefore, a symbol of democracy. However, the District's government is not a true democracy, shaped as it is by a compromise between the absolute jurisdiction of the Congress (as granted by the Constitution) and the democratic principle of self-government.

Washington, D.C., home to more than 622,600 people and encompassing more than 60 square miles of land area and 9 square miles of water area, is the seat of the federal government. However, D.C. residents, unlike other U.S. citizens, do not have voting representation in Congress; *taxation without representation still exists in the nation's capital.*

When the Congress, implementing its latest District reorganization, chartered the present city government in 1973, it retained the power to review (read: veto) legislation passed by the Council of the District of Columbia and to control city policy through a line-item veto review of the budget (the kind Congress won't give to the president). The new charter constrains the city's finances in that nonresident income is exempt from taxation (guess who benefits most from this?). This constraint exists despite the fact that all states, and most major cities, have the right to tax income earned in their jurisdiction by residents and nonresidents alike, even if only to cover the cost of city services provided to those income earners. Because 60 percent of all income earned in the District is by workers who live outside the city, this situation represents a serious stress on District finances.

Additionally, more than 41 percent of all District land is owned by the federal government and is therefore tax-exempt. Also, the District cannot impose real property taxes on certain privileged organizations favored by Congress. Chief among these are the Daughters of the American Revolution, the National Geographic Society, and the National Academy of Sciences. Furthermore, federal exemptions prohibit District taxation of the income of certain federal appointees, congressional representatives, and foreign residents. And the District is also prohibited from assessing road and bridge tolls.

What does all of this have to do with congressional privilege, you ask? Think about it. If you live in Connecticut, for example, but commute to work in Manhattan, under congressional ground rules you would pay no city income tax, no bridge or highway tolls on your daily commute, and no property taxes on your office space or equipment.

Considerably more funds are now available to dress up your personal work environment and improve both your personal and business bottom line, to say nothing about enhancing your fringe benefits.

A great deal, eh? Just change Connecticut to Alexandria or Silver Springs, for example, and change Manhattan to the District of Columbia—you get the picture.

Congress does provide some federal funding, claiming a major contribution toward covering D.C.'s expenses and offsetting those tax exemptions. Don't you believe it. In 1989 the mayor of the District of Columbia appointed a commission on budget and financial priorities, chaired by Dr. Alice M. Rivlin, of the Brookings Institution. This commission, equally funded by the federal and District governments, was charged with both evaluating the major causes of shortfall in budget revenues and recommending appropriate corrections.

HEED THE WARNING

The commission warned in its final report that the District government is facing an unprecedented period of insolvency unless the following actions are taken:

1. **Make the federal government contribute a larger share toward covering D.C.'s expenses.** Compared to the District's general fund revenue (GFR), Congress in 1989 contributed only 14.9 percent of the total. Down from a high of 19.55 percent in 1985, this number represented only a 1.3 percent increase in real dollars over a four-year period.
2. Provide for additional tax revenues by taxing non-residents who work in the District of Columbia.

The commission stated that "it believes the Federal government has treated the District of Columbia unfairly. It has imposed special costs on the District and severely restricted the District's revenue-raising capacity without paying adequate compensation."

PUNISHING THE PLAYGROUND

The commission believes that the federal government should be paying closer to 30 percent of the District's own source revenues and that payment should be a formula-based entitlement not subject to revocation or confiscation (the D.C. commissioners know their Congress). The commission also believes that their 30 percent recommendation has a better chance of passing than the alternative of Congress voting to subject itself and other nonresidents to a city income tax.

In granting limited District home rule, Congress was not acting out of generosity or even in the best interests of the District. Congress needed a scapegoat to avoid responsibility for another congressional boondoggle.

The congressional quid pro quo was to assign to the District government financial responsibility for pension plans Congress had established for police officers, firefighters, teachers, and judges. *At the time of this transfer, these plans were underfunded by nearly $3 billion.* In 1979, Congress enacted legislation requiring it to contribute $54.7 million toward that liability each year for 25 years. Simple arithmetic shows that this formula leaves the District responsible for funding the remaining 75 percent of a liability it did not incur.

Today that unfunded pension liability is estimated to be $5.4 billion and growing. This situation jeopardizes both the future security of thousands of District employees as well as the long-term solvency of the District's government.

In a similar manner, after granting the District limited home rule (always subject to congressional review), Congress forced the District to assume more than $300 million of an accumulated operating deficit. It is an established fact that bad management and poor financial decisions by the Congress, not by the District's government, are the primary causes of this deficit.

Also, Congress transferred St. Elizabeth's Hospital to the District in 1985 but never lived up to its commitment to fund capital improvements and correct cited safety deficiencies.

In closing its report, the commission stated that "it was appalled by the Federal Government's lack of fairness in its fiscal relationship with the District and appeals to the administration and Congress to rectify the situation." We can only hope that the commission is not holding its collective breath.

FINDING A SOLUTION

In examining the shambles left behind by the Congress in its partisan, self-serving micromanagement of the District's affairs, it doesn't take a rocket scientist to understand why the affairs of our nation are in a similar state. The same lack of intelligence and overt self-indulgence applied to the little District of Columbia is employed on a much grander scale in managing the affairs of the United States of America.

On November 6, 1990, the desperate voting residents of the District elected two "senators" and a "representative" to advocate before the Congress a petition by District residents for admission into the Union as the "State of New Columbia." These elected officials receive no salary, office support, or benefits from any appropriated funding source at this time.

District residents believe that only through statehood and its virtual autonomy from congressional interference can they free themselves from the oppressive political tampering of the Congress and begin to manage their own affairs effectively.

This latest action represents a continuation of a process that began in November 1980. Through the initiative process, the voting citizens of the District approved a law, the District of Columbia Statehood Constitutional Convention Act, that initiated a petition process (the Tennessee Plan) for statehood.

After hearings in the 100th Congress, H.R. 51, "a bill to provide for the admission of the State of New Columbia into the Union," was reported in the House by the Committee on the District of Columbia. No floor debate or votes were scheduled during that session of Congress.

Statehood bills have been before the Committee on the District of Columbia since the 92nd Congress (1971). They have received a great deal of lip service but no advancement. The voters of the District hope that the Tennessee Plan, which in some form has helped 17 states enter the Union, will ultimately bring success to their initiative.

In this plan, Tennessee (the first state to employ this tactic) provisionally elected two "senators" who were accorded seats on the Senate floor with speaking privileges for the purpose of advocating admission. Following Tennessee's triumphant strategy, the other petitioning territories to elect such officials were Michigan, Iowa, California, Oregon, Kansas, and Alaska. All these states successfully used the plan or a variant to gain statehood.

Residents of the District of Columbia can only hope that the example set by these territories will inure to their benefit. Of course, none of the territories was in the unenviable position of attempting to take away numerous privileges and conveniences from sitting members of the United States Congress.

POLICE POWER IN THE DISTRICT

Apart from the political tinkering that has been mentioned, how else do members of Congress gain benefits through the exercise of political power in the District?

Totally aside from its control over the District's purse strings, Congress exercises many unique oversight functions in its governance. Consider police authority, for example. Washington, D.C., has two public police forces among its many public law-enforcement agencies:

- **The United States Capitol Police Force (CPF)** is controlled by the Congress under the immediate direction of the Capitol Police Board, which consists of the Sergeant At Arms of the United States Senate, the Sergeant At Arms of the House of Representatives, and the Architect of the Capitol.

• **The Metropolitan Police Force (MPF)** reports to the mayor through the deputy mayor of operations.

The CPF's jurisdiction is anywhere the Congress authorizes. Specifically, CPF polices the Capitol's buildings and grounds and has jurisdiction over any areas with which the Architect of the Capitol has contracted, such as remote parking areas. This jurisdiction includes any area or street necessary to carry out its supervision and to travel between such areas and the Capitol. In this respect, the CPF has concurrent jurisdiction with the MPF.

Although members of the MPF are authorized to make arrests within the Capitol buildings and grounds, they are not authorized to enter these buildings except with the consent of or at the request of the Capitol Police Board. In case you are wondering, the word *grounds* does not mean just the lawn and walkways—it includes all buildings, office areas, parking areas, and spaces that are acquired or used by members of Congress or the Architect of the Capitol.

You can see why getting parking tickets fixed is a snap, especially when you control the police force. As far as more serious transgressions are concerned, members of Congress enjoy virtual sanctuary. The CPF for obvious reasons won't cite members, and the MPF is not empowered to get to them without obtaining prior jurisdictional permission. And you just know how quickly those patronage appointees, the Sergeants At Arms, are going to grant jurisdictional permission to the MPF.

For all practical purposes, the CPF has jurisdiction anywhere a member of Congress or staffer is likely to be found on a regular basis . . .the Washington National Airport, for example. A few years ago, if a certain powerful congressman had been a more frequent visitor to the tidal basin in Foggy Bottom, where his shapely companion chose to go swimming, he probably never would have been arrested. It pays to establish precedent in these matters.

DIVIDING UP THE DISTRICT

It is a sad commentary on our times that our nation's capital is perhaps the most unintegrated metropolis in the United States. And this situation is not limited specifically to race.

City politics and thus city patronage are completely dominated by the Democratic party, a reflection of more than 40 years of Democratic congressional majority. The mayor, congressional delegates, and every member of the District council (except for two) are Democrats. The only nonconformers are one Independent and one from the Statehood party. In effect, the District of Columbia has a one-party system.

The political boundaries of the District are also a reflection of the ethnic and racial composition that exists in our nation's capital. Of the eight political wards, each with a population range of between 73,400 and 80,900, only Ward 3, with the lowest population density in the city (16 persons per acre), has a preponderantly white population (86 percent), with 7 percent black and 7 percent other, of which 6 percent are estimated to be Latino.

Ward 3 has the highest assessed real-estate values in the city. It has no industrial acreage, and 89 percent of its single-family houses were assessed at $200,000 or more as of July 1989.

Every other ward, like the city itself, is predominantly black (67 percent, as opposed to 28 percent white, 6 percent Latino and 5 percent other), according to a 1986 household survey by the Greater Washington Research Center.

The purpose of these statistics is not to raise issues concerning racial or ethnic demographics but rather to illustrate again the abysmal failure of congressional stewardship in the District of Columbia. Its refusal to implement the fundamental civil and racial reforms it has imposed on the rest of the nation during the past 15 years is monstrous. Again and again, we find Congress exempting itself from the hard choices—the realities every American citizen must face on a daily basis.

LOOKING FOR SOLUTIONS

We find Congress repeatedly taking the easy (read: political) way out. It immerses itself in an orgy of self-indulgence and petty political backbiting and abrogates its responsibilities to direct the governance of the District impartially and with concern for the ultimate welfare of the District's citizens.

The District of Columbia is the most complex municipal government in the United States. It shares the qualities of a city, a state, and a federal protectorate and at the same time serves as the nation's capital. The District is also, sadly to say, a congressional administrative fiasco. Its growth and development—indeed, its ongoing operations—has been in most cases in spite of rather than because of the actions of the United States Congress.

We can only hope that the future of the District of Columbia will fulfill the vision of our forefathers and that this city will become a model of freedom and democracy—a shining example for others in the world to emulate and admire.

Perhaps for guidance in achieving this goal, the members of Congress should refer to the words of our first president, George Washington. He said, "It has always been my opinion, and still is so, that the administration of the affairs of the Federal city ought to be under the immediate direction of a judicious and skillful superintendent, . . . one in whom are united knowledge of men and things, industry, integrity, impartiality and firmness; and that this person should reside on the spot."

8

Undeserving Grandfathers: Typical Campaign-Financing Flimflammery

Nineteen ninety-two was a banner year for the election of freshman congresspersons to the hallowed House of Representatives. Not since the great turnover, when Eisenhower was swept into office, have so many new faces been seen on the floor of the House.

Was this the result of some massive electoral reform movement? Perhaps it was the coattail impact of a popular new president sweeping his followers to victory. This is hardly the case, despite myriad legitimate reasons for change. It was just Congress doing business as usual— exploiting privilege to stuff its personal pocketbook at taxpayers' expense.

LEAVING WITH THE SURPLUS

It's shameful enough that members of Congress are
allowed to fill huge campaign war chests with contributions from special interests (who raise these funds by
socking it to their clients in the form of higher prices),
but the House of Representatives compounds that
shame. How? It uses an obscure grandfather clause that
permitted senior members who chose to retire in 1992 to
transfer unused funds to their personal bank accounts.

*If they elected to leave office at the end of their term in 1992,
165 House members could have pocketed more than $41 million
in leftover campaign money.*

When Congress finally outlawed the personal use of
surplus campaign funds in 1979, the House added some
small print (when something is really wrong, it can always
be found in the small print of an obscure clause). This
addition "exempted" the incumbents who approved the
reform—all members elected before 1980. The House
then repealed that loophole in a new ethics bill ten years
later. However, true to form, the House created yet
another grandfather clause that benefits all members
who retire or lose an election by 1993 (an unsurprising
and predictable consistency).

A study by the Center for Public Integrity (CPI), a
Washington, D.C., nonprofit research group, found that
House members amassed these "golden parachutes"
because most had such weak opponents (if any) that they
barely used their campaign treasuries to win reelection.
This study sadly reflects on the success of various congressional programs that virtually guarantee incumbent
reelection.

These 165 lawmakers (111 Democrats and 54 Republicans, who make up more than one-third of the House)
now have seniority. Some of them, contrary to the nature
of most politicians, may choose not to leave office just for

the money—and the accompanying negative publicity. After all, after you have raised your cash cow, it pays to milk it for a while.

The common rationale for continuing to accumulate these enormous war chests was, and continues to be, the hypothetical future appearance of a multimillionaire opponent willing to spend vast resources on an election challenge that the unwealthy incumbent will be required to counter. However, the CPI also said that the money was often "destined for other than campaign purposes."

These sums are not unsubstantial. Larry Hopkins (R-KY), has about $600,000 in his campaign treasury; Doug Barnard, Jr. (D-GA), has about $580,000. Stephen J. Solarz, a Brooklyn Democrat, tops the list with nearly $1.4 million, and 20 others have more than half a million dollars—hardly a pittance.

It pays to remember that people make a campaign contribution to help defray necessary expenses incurred during the course of a political campaign for public office. They fully expect these funds to be used to offset marketing and advertising expenses, pay the salaries of non-volunteer staff, and in the case of statewide office seekers (senate and governor, for example), airfares, taxis, and car rentals. No one makes a political contribution in the expectation that it will find its way into a candidate's pocket to ease his "golden years."

Additionally, contributions are frequently made because of political conviction rather than because of the candidate personally. Constituents want to emphasize a particular cause or political philosophy and expect their contributions to be used to further these ends.

However, incumbents nationwide routinely take advantage of weak election laws which require only that campaign funds be used for a political purpose. Notwithstanding the clear intent of these laws, many politicians view these contributions as an enhancement to their lifestyle and ultimate retirement.

It is true that some former members of Congress have donated their excess funds for such purposes as establishing college endowments, giving to charities, and support-ing other, less well-funded campaigns of former political allies. Many others, however, have given new meaning to the definition of "political purposes."

Representatives have purchased lavish banquets, airfare, expensive wines and liquors, and door prizes; taken staff members on summer retreats; stored personal belongings; and bought paintings, office equipment, new automobiles, and gifts, gifts, and more gifts. Robert E. Badham (R-CA), spent more than $40,000 in leftover campaign money for such items as personal travel, formal wear, jewelry for his wife, club dues, and dry cleaning.

TAXING THE SURPLUS

Representatives are not alone in dipping into campaign coffers. As reported in the *Washington Post* in September 1989, "a vaguely worded provision inserted by Senate Republicans into last year's tax law allows election campaign contributions to be spent for Senators' office costs—from dry cleaning to new cars to foreign travel—*free of federal income tax!*"

This provision is a reversal of longstanding tax law and Internal Revenue Service policy. The IRS has stated in two rulings concerning office expenses that transfers from campaign funds for this purpose were subject to a 34 percent tax.

Tax lawyers who discovered this obscure provision decry this blatant attempt to transfer campaign funds to personal use to avoid the payment of tax.

According to campaign reports to the Federal Election Commission, one of the major beneficiaries, the National Republican Senatorial Committee (NRSC), without benefit of this provision would have had to pay taxes on millions of dollars the committee spends for senators' noncampaign costs, including thousands of dollars worth of interviews recorded in the Senate's private television station and broadcast by satellite to local television news programs.

Democratic senators receive no such aid from their election committee; but instead, they have personally used leftover campaign funds to cover noncampaign expenses despite the Senate rule prohibiting members from using any campaign funds for personal use while in office or after they depart.

Senator Bill Bradley (D-NJ), for example, spent $1,111 in campaign funds on a trip to Switzerland; Senator Spark Matsunaga (D-HI) bought a $27,000 Cadillac; and Finance Committee Chairman Senator Lloyd Bentsen (D-TX) spent $8,267 for his use of the Senate recording studio.

Like many of the tax provisions with special-interest beneficiaries, this one is couched in obscure language. It does not mention senators or their campaign committees. The law, as described in a congressional report, is termed a "conforming change," which is legalese that allows elective officeholders to be reimbursed for their expenses without tax penalty.

It is noteworthy that Senate Republicans made two attempts (in 1986 and 1987) to insert this tax exemption before succeeding in 1988. It is also noteworthy that the Senate made no attempt to include the House membership in the rules change. And as a final comment about the public merit of this provision, consider that it was inserted into the new tax law without congressional debate and without the submission of IRS opinions.

THE EFFECTS OF STASHING YOUR SURPLUS

This book does not get into the sticky wicket of campaign-financing reform; indeed, that subject deserves a
book of its own. The egregious impact of the current
system, however, is worthy of some illustration and limited commentary.

*By November 1992, private interests had paid more than $1
billion to buy the Congress of their choice!* This statement
means that private interests and PAC contributors have
acquired veto power on key committees over proposals
that threaten them and their projects. According to a
January 28, 1993, op-ed piece in the *New York Times* by
Joseph A. Califano, Jr., the former secretary of health,
education, and welfare, and domestic affairs assistant to
President Johnson from 1965 to 1969, these "interests
spent $314 million for the 1992 House elections and
$581 million on the elections [1988, 1990, and 1992]
that produced the current Senate. . . . Back-door support
and money raised by political parties added at least $100
million."

So long as they need private financing for future campaigns, these elected officials are unlikely to slap the
hands that feed them, much less get into a bare-knuckled
fight with their political action committees. So long as
private money clogs the arteries of political power, any
major reform package will include payoffs to special
interests.

As an example, Lyndon Johnson, the only modern
president with the political strength and savvy to drive
major health reform through Congress, still had to pay
the private pipers.

In 1964, according to Califano, Johnson couldn't get
the Senate Finance or House Ways and Means committees to move his bill. Late that year, he garnered sufficient votes on the Senate floor to attach Medicare to a

House bill that raised Social Security benefits, but the House refused to accept the Senate version.

Thus to obtain popular pressure for the increase for Medicare, Johnson killed the Social Security bill shortly before the 1964 elections. He then won the '64 election by the greatest landslide in U.S. history and carried into office a 2-to-1 Democratic majority in the House and a public mandate for his programs. In spite of this, to structure a House Ways and Means Committee majority for Medicare and Medicaid, LBJ was forced to abandon the authority his bill gave the government to set medical reimbursement rates.

The medical lobby had the power to compel the president to agree to pay doctors "reasonable," "customary," and "prevailing" fees—something the commercial insurers had refused to do because it gave physicians unlimited power to raise their own fees.

Recognizing the peril to the cost structure of the fledgling health-care system, LBJ pressed to change the payment system. He predicted that, without action, health costs would reach $100 billion by 1975. Pressured by industry lobbyists, Congress failed to act, and by 1975 health-care costs exceeded $133 billion. Today these costs are approaching three-quarters of a trillion dollars!

When the compelling priority in Washington, D.C.— reelection—is coupled with the problems in our current campaign-finance system (skyrocketing campaign costs with excessive dependence on special-interest contributors), their undue influence on our politicians is magnified. Because of the candidates' intense need to raise enormous sums of money to guarantee reelection (senators raise an average of $12,000 each week and House incumbent spending has doubled since 1982), special-interest groups and lobbyists with unlimited access to millions of dollars are capable of buying a Congress of their choice.

With new leadership in the executive branch and more than 120 new members of Congress who campaigned on the need for change, it would seem that we have a historic opportunity to clean up Congress and rid Washington of the corrupting influence of special-interest money. Public outrage requires that action occur quickly and that changes be more than cosmetic. Still, the prospects for reform remain dim until the stranglehold that special-interest groups have on many key members of Congress is finally broken.

SUGGESTIONS FOR REFORM

Comprehensive reform clearly must include these four key elements:

- **Spending limits**
- **Drastic reductions in individual and PAC contributions**
- **Significant public contributions**
- **A ban on soft-money donations** (monies given to political parties or voter-registration drives rather than to a specific candidate)

The key challenge is to drive special-interest money out of politics and replace it with untainted, alternative resources.

Congressional elections in 1992 added more than 100 of America's privileged class to the leisure class, who chose to forgo the halls of Congress and the hustle-bustle of our nation's capital. They have returned to their respective homes, to travel, golf, and fish and otherwise enjoy the fruits of their labors in contented retirement.

These ex-members of Congress are enriched both by the fond memories of a life spent in public service and by a bank account overflowing with surplus campaign funds for which no legitimate use was ever identified.

9

Congressional Seniority: Preserving the Old-Boy Network

Two primal forces are inherent in members of the United States Congress. The first is self-preservation. Considered to be the most basic instinct of homo sapiens, among politicians this instinct translates into "get reelected at all costs." Nothing else is more important. This primal force pervades the political psyche and manifests itself in every emotion, thought, and deed.

The second primal instinct is power, evidenced by the driving need of members of Congress to become *primus inter pares*, or "the first among equals." As envisioned by our Founding Fathers, all are equals, and none rule. This concept is exemplified in the three independent branches of government, each subject to appropriate checks and balances.

Congress's egalitarian structure was established to promote comradeship and a spirit of cooperation among the membership. Our country's founders envisioned governance by means of negotiation and compromise, with resolution achieved through reason and persuasion without benefit of separate power bases. Thus all decisions were made for the benefit of the country, not for individuals or groups. The Founding Fathers envisioned dedicated public servants—representatives without hidden agendas who serve only one master, their constituency. In their wildest dreams, it probably never occurred to them that holding political office would become the goal in itself or that a new order of priorities would place public service to one's country at the end of a very long list.

This concept is certainly altruistic, but remember that these men had just created a new country and had given everything in its cause. After such sacrifice, how could they possibly have anticipated the corrupt greediness of the political hordes that followed?

After the new politicians were elected, their first order of business was to create a comprehensive set of rules and mechanisms under which the new Congress would operate. Twisting the intent and concepts of our Founding Fathers to their own ends, they established *a privileged class*. Never content with the status quo, each succeeding Congress contributed its bit with the two primal forces motivating their actions—how to best ensure their own reelection and acquire power.

The former objective has been discussed at length in preceding chapters. A success rate of more than 90 percent in the reelection of incumbents is abundant testimony to the progress achieved in that endeavor.

CREATING THE SENIORITY SYSTEM

But how do you create a pecking order in the chicken coop? A worrisome question? Not really. Congress simply turned to an ancient ploy used by bureaucracies throughout the centuries. It created a seniority system and resolved to process all legislative business by committee.

Each party selected (by seniority) a few individuals who would serve as the party's spokespersons, floor managers, and so on. It was agreed that the majority party would have first choice in the distribution of goodies, such as committee chairmanships, office locations, and parking privileges (you know—the really important stuff needed to run a country). Individual priorities were adjudicated solely on the basis of length of term in office.

It makes no difference whatsoever that the seniority system has been thoroughly discredited. Governments from time immemorial have seen their enterprises stifled, their energies dissipated, and critical operations stymied because of the gridlock of power structures created by a seniority system.

Even the class-conscious military forgoes its cherished seniority in times of crisis in favor of talent and inspirational leadership. When Dwight D. Eisenhower was made supreme commander of all allied forces in Europe, he was promoted over the heads of 42 senior officers.

Never mind that a seniority system punishes creativity and individual enterprise. Never mind that all endeavor is reduced to the lowest common denominator with priorities and decision-making possible at only the most senior level. Never mind that a seniority system is anathema to the democratic process, subverting all else to the hour and date that one assumes office. Never mind because a seniority system is the one absolutely essential step necessary to create *a privileged class*.

Time in office equates to power as surely as $e=mc^2$. Tenure means control of committee chairmanships, and that means control of legislative agendas, and that begets trading power, patronage priority, leverage, prestige, and perks, perks, and more perks.

The more time spent in office, the higher one rises in the political hierarchy, the more favors one can bestow, and the more IOUs one can collect. Senior members of Congress garner more pork for the folks back home, which increases the home-base political clout, which converts to a bigger campaign war chest and ultimately all the money one needs to beat any reelection threat (or perhaps retire to a life of leisure luxury).

A seniority system creates hierarchy, which by one definition is "government by an elite group"—or *a privileged class.*

Hierarchies breed special-interest groups, PACS, and other organizations that promote their activities through the disbursement of huge sums of money, both directly and indirectly, to lawmakers in powerful positions. Eager to sustain this advantage and to promote their image as power brokers—real movers and shakers—the lawmakers form cliques whose sole purpose is to trade political favors among themselves. The cliques in turn form alliances with other cliques and thus is born the "old-boy network," which in one way or another now controls the future of all legislation in the United States Congress.

The old-boy network is self-sustaining; it feeds itself through patronage, favoritism, and the control of huge campaign war chests whose proceeds are disbursed to needy incumbents by the powerful few in control. Need new legislation introduced? A pork-barrel subsidy? A special project for the folks at home? Do you need to fend off a rich challenger or perhaps promote a protégé's campaign in another congressional district? Well, then, you have to belong. It's easy—just sell your integrity and become "one of the boys." Do as you are told, and you will have the bucks available to buy the votes. Your constituents will never know, (only 40 to 50 percent of them vote, anyway).

PUTTING SENIORITY INTO PRACTICE

As an example of the seniority system in action, for more years than anyone could remember, Congressman Les Aspin was the chairman of the powerful House Armed Services Committee. An expert on military matters, he worked closely with his Senate counterpart, Senator Sam Nunn, and together (both are Democrats) they effectively guided legislation for Republican administrations to create the finest military force in world history. Their efforts had a significant impact on the dissolution of the Soviet Union. At the end of the Cold War, following administration policies, Aspin and Nunn recognized the need to reduce the size of the military and bring it into line with the nation's current needs.

With the election of a new president, Aspin was chosen to be the new secretary of defense and left his House committee to the not-so-tender mercies of the senior Democratic House member, Representative Ron Dellums (D-CA). I say "not-so-tender" because Dellums is a man with an unparalleled history of obstructionism and anti-military bias. His apparent sole purpose for being on the committee was to be the peacenik fly in the Pentagon ointment. He was the spoiler—a man who, if left to his own devices, would forgo any U.S. military presence in favor of radical, liberal, domestic programs.

Dellums, on record as embracing Fidel Castro's brand of Communism, brags of his intent to shut down our intelligence agencies and reduce the U.S military to a state of impotence. His sole qualification to serve on this committee is that he is a charter member of the old-boy network who has acquired lifetime job tenure, thanks to superior pork-barreling proficiency for his district.

Dellums, through seniority alone, without regard for ability, dedication, knowledge of military matters, or even

administrative skill, now chairs one of the most powerful
and influential committees in the House. This committee, whose primary responsibility is the defense of the
United States, is now under the direction of a man whose
allegiance to this country can be seriously questioned.
Ron Dellums is just another one of the good ol' boys.

BREAKING THE SENIORITY STRANGLEHOLD

Can this stranglehold be broken? You bet! For example,
among the freshmen members of Congress are two senators from California: Diane Feinstein and Barbara Boxer.
Although these two women were in the same election,
through a quirk in the election law, Feinstein was sworn
into office a month before Boxer. Feinstein's Senate victory swept out of office a man appointed to fill then-Sen-
ator Pete Wilson's unexpired term when he left the Senate to become the governor of California (he had
defeated Feinstein for that position).

The law stipulates that the winner of a regular election
for an electoral office held by an appointee can take
office immediately after that election (and before the
current term expires) rather than wait for installation at
the beginning of the new term. The purpose is to get a
seniority jump on all new members being sworn in at the
beginning of their new term.

Thus Feinstein became the new senior senator from
California and is entitled to all the advantages the position entails. One advantage is priority in making recommendations for state judgeships, civil commissioners, and
appointees to military academies.

To Feinstein's credit, she invited Boxer to participate
equally in this process. Perhaps this courtesy was
extended because they are both Democratic women in a
mostly male environment, or perhaps Feinstein wanted

to enlist a supporter for her reelection in two years. This departure from the norm raised many eyebrows in the old-boy network, whose participants were more used to competition than cooperation. Could it be that this example represents the first crack in the dam? It is certainly an example worth emulating.

A ROTATING SOLUTION

Can such a pernicious system be stopped? Absolutely. To ensure that all legislators get an equal opportunity to serve their country first and special interests last and to guarantee that public service does not become a banquet at the public trough, why not rotate committee chairmanships?

This process could work as follows. First, institute term limits to prevent the rotation from becoming a game of musical chairs among senior members. Then limit the chairmanship to one term of two years every four years. During the alternating years, the committee chairs simply become committee members. No member is allowed to serve more than four consecutive years on the same committee. Fresh blood brings fresh ideas.

Thus a senator, limited to two terms, could conceivably be a chairperson, if found qualified by their colleagues, for 6 of any 12 years served. A senator could serve twice on the same committee, but a 4-year interval would occur between each service. The probable scenario is 4 years on, 4 years off, and then 4 years on again as the chairperson the last 2 years of the last term. House members would fare the same, assuming term limits of 6 terms each and their subsequent reelection.

Because most members serve on multiple committees, it is likely that veteran members will garner a wealth of experience in multiple areas of government and sacrifice only their ability to establish powerful personal fiefdoms in the process. The real winners would be their constituents, who will no longer have to battle the well-heeled, organized special-interest groups for the services of their elected representatives.

This system would eliminate the spectacle of powerful members (such as former Speaker Jim Wright) conducting their own foreign policy adventures over the objections of both the State Department and the president.

The rotation of committee chairs and the constant infusion of fresh members is a system that would work and work well. It is time to give the Congress back to the people.

10

Why Sir Galahad Is Leaving Camelot and Stopping the Gravy Train

In 1993, 110 members of Congress did not return to those hallowed halls. Were they voted out of office? Hardly. The majority simply chose, for a variety of reasons, not to seek reelection.

REASONS FOR LEAVING

For many, the reason was purely financial. Having milked the cash cow long enough and while still eligible for a fat retirement bonus payoff in unspent campaign funds, it was time to vamoose or, to quote Woody Allen, "Take the money and run."

For others, however, the reasons for leaving were more profound and personal and had more to do with how

their attitudes toward public service were changed by
their experiences in Washington.

Some of the more common reasons put forth by retiring members in a *Time* magazine interview.

On campaign financing, *Time* magazine Democratic
Senator Tim Wirth of Colorado said, "Congress is awash
in money. Interests have emerged that have enormous
amounts of cash and that [they] stand between the Congress and its constituency . . . I have seen the denominator of debate get lower and lower, and I think much of
that is explained by fear—fear that you will be unable to
raise money from a certain group; or worse, that the
interest group will give the money to the other guy; or
worse still, that the money will go to a third party as a
so-called independent expenditure . . . We need reform
that would do three things: provide shared public-private
funding, similar to the current system for presidential
campaigns; second, limit how much a candidate can
spend; and third, ensure non-incumbents of enough
money to be competitive—which would, by the way,
ensure better members of Congress."

Participating in the same interview, Republican Congressman Vin Weber had this observation: "I think the
impact of special-interest groups is greater [especially]
when they are organizing voters in your district . . . Their
ability to organize makes them more of a power than the
amount of [any] check they might write."

Another participant in the interview, Democratic Senator Kent Conrad, of North Dakota, feels that the real
problem is time, or rather, the lack of it: "People ask me
why the Senate seems to always come out at night to vote
. . . The answer is because nobody's got time during the
day. You have endless meetings and endless demands:
speeches, appearances, getting your picture taken with
the kids from back home."

Senator Wirth addressed the problem of leadership in
Congress: "All of us are entrepreneurs. The leadership

has no handle on us. They can't really do anything for us or to us. So the place gets more horizontally structured, and every time we have a vote, [Senate Majority Leader] George Mitchell's got to get on his horse and try to round up 57 heifers, who are in pastures all over the place. The leadership has no power anymore."

Weber said, "I think the erosion of the political parties is to blame for much of what's wrong. Certainly, parties were once corrupt and needed reform. But now they are unable to play the role they *should* play—as filters between special-interest groups and individual office-holders . . ."

"We are separate operators," Conrad said. "We raise our own money. . . . The balkanization of Congress [weakens leadership] when you've got to refer a bill to nine separate committees on the House side . . . I mean, how do you ever get through the process? The media bears substantial responsibility . . . Journalists have gone from a healthy skepticism to a destructive cynicism . . . I think the media fails to deal with substance in favor of any minor scandal that comes along."

Weber believes, "The best reform you can have is to say nobody can contribute to a candidate except an individual or a political party." Conrad adds, "The problem is the amount of money in the campaigns." Wirth's conclusion is, "The reason why these people get entrenched in the House is that the disparities of money are so huge."

However, when Wirth was asked a direct question in another interview about why he chose not to run for reelection, he responded that it was partisan pettiness, legislative gridlock, and the "hysterical superficiality" of television.

Weber has said that the prospect of dragging his family through a "vicious, negative, and highly personal campaign" in which his opponent would have accused him of writing bad checks was his reason for leaving Congress.

Perhaps closer to the truth is a quote from Representative Jerry Lewis (R-Redlands) a seven-term Congressman and the third-ranking Republican leader in the House. He described the legislative environment this way: "It's almost a pall hanging over the place . . . It's a negative mood so thick you could cut it with a knife." In agreement is Representative Fred Grandy (R-IA), who called it "a time of fear and frustration."

At the time of these interviews, 44 House members (29 Democrats and 15 Republicans) had announced they would not seek reelection, with the number expected to exceed the postwar record of 49 voluntary departures. The record for House turnovers was 118 members in 1949.

In the Senate, the seven retirements announced so far are just above average for an election year. However, it is considered remarkable that this list includes a number of rising, highly respected, younger members, a phenomenon duplicated in the House.

Why? Among the grievances are a growing sense of anger at what many characterize as the media's trivialization of the political process and the often demeaning demands placed on candidates, who must raise enormous sums of money to run for political office.

The job does seem to lack charisma, based on a combination of dissatisfaction in the inability of a bloated congressional bureaucracy to break the gridlock that ties up important legislation, frustration over the end result of divided government in which neither party can truly govern, and despair over the low esteem in which the public holds Congress.

Many lawmakers privately complain that the public is uninvolved, uninformed, and unrealistic about what it can expect from a government that lacks the popular mandate to enact real and necessarily painful reforms.

None, however, publicly admits to advocating a political system that encourages gross economic mismanagement, panders to partisan pettiness, and engages in relentless and pointless political maneuvering that has stymied the Congress, created a budget that is out of control, crippled the economy, and prevented a president from leading the country.

Representative Lewis cites a "confluence of factors that in combination are going to produce a major turnover," and Representative Henry Waxman (D-CA) blames frustration and abuse.

Perhaps getting closest to the truth in an interview excerpted from the L.A. Times, retiring Republican San Diego Congressman Lowery reflected on his 12 years in the House with these comments about the House power structure: "I think you have three problems . . . The Republicans for three decades have had a virtual lock on the presidency—Jimmy Carter was an aberration. The Democrats have had a virtual lock on Congress going back about five decades. This has caused tremendous tension because of the differences in philosophies and priorities and approaches. The second problem relates to Congress and the fact that 136 committee chairmen—over half of the Democratic caucus—have their own little fiefdoms. There has been a diffusion of power, to the point where its very, very difficult to govern. The other internal problem is the short shrift given to the minority . . . The deck is stacked before we even begin to discuss an issue. Unfair minority ratios on committees, coupled with the diffusion of power among the majority, has been a prescription for disaster. And you add that on top of this war that's been going on with the executive branch, and its no wonder that the American public is getting frustrated, because there is not a whole lot of work getting done here."

Lowery responded to a question about what changes he would propose to make the House work better: "A balanced-budget amendment would go a long way. Giving the executive [President] authority for the line-item

veto would help. Even doing something as simple as an
enhanced rescission . . . that the savings proposed by a
President would be automatic unless Congress overruled
them."

This profound and thoughtful insight from some of
the many who have spent years toiling in the Congressional brair patch barely scratches the surface.

Consider the frustration of Senator Warren Rudman
(R-NH) who finally got fed up with the refusal of his
colleagues to face up to the biggest overdraft of all: a
$400 billion budget deficit. According to sources familiar
with Rudman's presidential aspirations, he desperately
wanted to distance himself from the congressional can of
worms. After all, the last sitting senator to win the presidential election was John F. Kennedy, when the country
was in the middle of a postwar boom.

STOPPING THE GRAVY TRAIN
WITH A LINE-ITEM VETO

So how do we change the system and cut the fat from the
bloated congressional hog? I suggest that we begin by
listening very carefully to the people who have been
there. Between the lines of their public remarks lies the
true course of our salvation.

For example. Every president in this century has asked
Congress to give him line-item veto power—to no avail.
This power would give the president the authority to
strike billions of dollars of wasteful spending from budget bills—to really cut the fat (an anathema to all dedicated politicians).

With Republican chief executives, the Democrat-con-
trolled Congress blocked the line-item veto by arguing
that the issue was a partisan power grab. With a Demo-

cratic chief executive, the debate must now be waged on the merits of the line-item veto.

Although opponents charge that the veto would not have any impact on federal deficit spending, one objective way to measure its effectiveness as a budget tool is to examine its impact at the state level.

To fund the federal government, Congress passes only 13 major spending bills a year. Each of these gigantic appropriations confronts the president with a "like it or lump it" choice: Either veto the entire bill, which can result in the closure of entire agencies (such as the Department of Defense), or sign it and drive taxpayers deeper into debt.

The governors of 43 states have some form of constitutional line-item veto authority. The Cato Institute, a Washington, D.C. think tank, recently conducted a survey to examine the effectiveness of these states' line-item vetoes. They discovered that 90 percent of the governors categorized the tool as either "useful" or "very useful" in balancing the budget. Fully 92 percent recommended that the president have that authority. In this bipartisan recommendation, 90 percent of the Democratic governors support the proposal.

The governor of Wisconsin, for example, has used this tool 1,300 times to save his state's taxpayers more than $150 million. In Michigan, Governor John Engler's judicious use of the veto helped him to avoid raising taxes during his recession-torn state's terrible financial crisis.

Kansas Governor Joan Finney (D) defines the problem this way: "Just as I have direct accountability to the entire state, while the legislators (each) report to a relatively small constituency, so the President must account to the entire nation as Members of Congress respond to the needs of 535 varying constituencies."

It is no secret that many members are strongly opposed to the line-item veto precisely because it would prevent such abuses as the $5 billion in pork projects inserted in the 1990 comprehensive highway authorization bill. These designated "demonstration projects" included a parking garage in Chicago, an exit ramp to an amusement park in Ohio, and bicycle paths in California.

WASTE, WASTE, AND MORE WASTE

Pork-barrel spending is traditionally targeted not on the basis of priority and need but on the basis of political clout.

Under current budget rules, no matter how desirable a program may be, the White House cannot prevent the powerful chairman of the Senate Appropriations Committee (Senator Robert Byrd, of West Virginia) from channeling a lion's share of new grants and aid to Charleston, Morgantown, and Wheeling.

Byrd, for example, decided that the nation needed a third "master clock" to tell the exact time. It doesn't matter that we already have two "master clocks" and don't need a third clock (let alone the backup) any longer, according to the Naval Observatory's scientific director, the nation's timekeeper. Despite the director's recommendation, Senator Byrd wants it, and he wants it where else—in West Virginia. He is even willing to spend $7 million of the taxpayers' money to get it.

Lest you think that Byrd is alone in his relentless search for pork to feed his constituency, consider Senator Ted Stevens' (R-AL) project to provide a supercomputer to the University of Alaska for auroras borealis energy research.

Researchers, such as the director of the American Physical Society's Washington, D.C office, have defined the idea as "wacky," with colleagues estimating that getting even a minute amount of energy from auroras would entail using an antenna thousands of miles in length.

In spite of this, Stevens offered an amendment to the Energy Department's appropriations bill to determine which supercomputer would be required. He skipped the normal peer review process, and his amendment was adopted without debate or a roll-call vote. The Defense Appropriations Subcommittee, on which he is the ranking Republican, earmarked $25 million to fund the program.

Atmospheric scientists were shocked by the legislation. The University of Alaska, unwilling to look a gift horse in the mouth, tried to justify the supercomputer as a tool for monitoring global environmental change, even though it admittedly had no need for such a powerful device.

To jam this project into the budget, Stevens took advantage of a joint House and Senate Appropriations Committee meeting to include it among $6 billion worth of similar projects that bloat the defense-funding bills— projects that had either never been authorized or had never been peer reviewed or open to competitive bidding. Normally, laws require competition for federal research dollars; the conference committee simply suspended this requirement.

It is interesting that other outraged lawmakers categorized this as an egregious example of pork-barrel politics, not as good government. Could it be that envy raised its ugly head?

Since becoming chairman of the House Appropriations Committee in 1979, Representative Jamie Whitten (D-MS), elected in 1941, one month before Pearl Harbor, has been freely lavishing his district with gifts paid for by taxpayers. One of his latest gifts is a $3 billion solid-rocket project the space program doesn't need, the Administration doesn't want to fund, and no one seems able to stop. This striking example shows the pork-barrel-producing power of the longest-serving member of Congress.

Whitten's plan required relocating of 300 employees from California (the site of two Advanced Solid-Rocket Motor [ASRM] plants) to Yellow Creek, Mississippi. This location was mandated despite the fact that the 126-foot-tall solid rockets would have to be shipped by barge 300 miles from Yellow Creek to the Stennis Space Station in Bay St. Louis, Mississippi, for test firing. It didn't matter that the need for these rockets was long gone, because NASA was so pleased with the redesign of the older models it had ordered 142 of them, enough to last through the year 2000.

Alarmed by the runaway costs associated with this project, an additional $401 million in 1991 and $465 million more in 1992, the Office of Management and Budget (OMB) tried to kill the ASRM program, and the highly regarded National Academy of Sciences wants the program reexamined. Undeterred, Whitten is attempting to find $480 million more for ASRM using his committee.

Consider the projects in this list:

$205,000 spent for a theater project in Cleveland

$50,000 for seedless-grapes research in Arkansas

$4.4 million for a railroad crossing "demonstration project" in Springfield, Illinois

$1 million for a National Bicycling and Walking Study

$250,000 for sweet-potato research

$150,000 on sweet-potato whiteflies

$100,000 on soybean ink

$200,000 for locoweed research in New Mexico

$8 million for a pedestrian bridge in Portland, Oregon

The grand prize goes for the $250,000 spent in determining the rectal temperature of hibernating bears in Alaska.

None of us should be grateful for this. These projects illustrate that anything is fair game in the name of serving your district (otherwise known as "get yourself reelected at all costs") as long as it spends money in your district. This foolishness goes on daily in Congress, and you, the taxpayer, are footing the bill.

SUGGESTIONS FOR LASTING REFORM

Now that you know the magnitude of and reasons for the problems, specific remedies for derailing the gravy train promptly suggest themselves, especially in light of what has been discussed in these pages and what professional students of good government have been clamoring for during the past 20 years.

1. **The President must be given line-item veto power** to eliminate waste. In this same context, presidential impoundment authority (the authority not to spend appropriated money when the expenditure is no longer viewed as being in the public interest) should be restored.

   For the past two decades, budgetary power has tilted away from the president and toward an imperial Congress. In the early 1970s, Congress rescinded the president's impoundment power. It is no accident that the era of $100 billion, then $200 billion, and now $300 billion deficits began when Congress seized the federal purse strings from the White House.

2. **Enact a Constitutional balanced-budget amendment** with emergency funding limited exclusively to

national defense. Many members of Congress recognize and endorse the need for outside interven-
tion. As Senator John McCain (R-AZ) puts it: "We
lack discipline, we are spending addicts, and we
can't admit it. We can't 'just say no.' We need
help."

3. **Enact term limits for all members of Congress**.
   Only by eliminating the old-boy network and making the national interest—not personal reelection—the first priority can we ensure that national
   interests will prevail.

   Already 15 states, with 30 percent of all Senate
   seats and 36 percent of all House seats, have
   imposed limits on their senators and representatives, and more of this type of legislation is in the
   works. This battle must be conducted on a state-by-
   state basis because Tom Foley and the Democratic
   Barons of the House refuse to permit a constitutional term-limit amendment to come to a floor
   vote. Members of the old-boy network are terrified
   of voting on a measure that might be fatal to their
   careers if it is enacted and, that because more than
   70 percent of the public favors such an amendment, could also be fatal to their careers if they kill
   it on the floor.

   The constitutional term-limit amendments are
   now suffocating in the House Judiciary Committee,
   chaired by Jack Brooks (D-TX), who was elected
   when Arthur Godfrey was only on radio and the
   Atlanta Braves called Boston home. In the more
   liberal Senate, support for term limits is increasing.
   In a 1948 vote these limits received only one vote,
   in 1991 they got 30, and in 1993 they received 39.

   This grass-roots movement is one of the broadest-
   based in the nation. The answer to the question,
   "Where most recently have term limits passed?" is

"Wherever most recently people were permitted to vote on them."

4. **Congress must not exclude itself from any legislation it passes.** This discrepancy should be corrected immediately with a law placing Congress under the authority of all existing prior exempted legislation. Congress survived beautifully until 1933 without exempting itself from any of the legislation it passed. The pseudo-argument that the Constitution requires exemption is as fallacious as it is superficial. There is no justification, unless one wishes only to cite privilege.

5. **Congress and officials in the White House must set the example for reform and sacrifice by eliminating all perks and special privileges,** except those mandated by national-security considerations (for example, Air Force One). In this context, administrative and Congressional salaries should be cut by 10 percent and their retirement plans reduced to bring them in line with those of the public sector. Salary increases should be eliminated until deficit spending has been eliminated and a realistic program for reduction of the national debt been enacted.

6. **Laws must be passed to eliminate all possibilities of special interests giving huge sums of money to candidates.** In this regard, all foreign lobbying should be made illegal and the role of domestic lobbyists reduced to that of providing only information, not money directly or indirectly.

7. **Campaign-financing reform must limit contributions exclusively to individuals and national political parties.** No political action committees and soft-money contributions to campaigns should be allowed. All funds not spent in the campaign process should be used to help offset the office expen-

ditures of the victorious candidate. No monies should be carried over to other elections or be used for personal expenditures of any sort not relating to the actual campaign.

8. **A limit must be imposed on campaign expenditures.** Because a limit on the funds that can be donated by an individual could be considered unconstitutional, campaigns must have time limits. They should be limited to six weeks before any election for regional and local contests, and ten weeks before national elections. A nationwide primary should be established for presidential elections. The electoral college should also be replaced with the popular vote to preclude manipulation of the presidential election, because a simple majority in only nine states can secure victory no matter what the popular-vote majority is.

9. **Statehood should be granted to Washington, D.C., with all the rights and privileges accorded to any state in the union.** This national seat of government's federal operations should in no way be infringed by this arrangement, and its activities should be supported by a budget mutually agreed on between the state and the Congress.

Although not addressed specifically in this book, one of the great failings in congressional operations is obviously the lack of planning, management expertise, testing, and accountability to the people regarding specific national programs enacted by Congress.

Business leaders worldwide subscribe to fundamental principles in the conduct of their enterprise. Any country that wants to achieve a sound fiscal basis to sustain its economy must do likewise. Applications of these principles should incorporate the following suggestions:

• **Any major budgetary program should include an overall plan that enunciates specific spending cuts,**

government restructuring, spending increases, and subsequent tax or revenue increases, with the projected net result presented to the people *before any tax increases are enacted.* Programmed revenue targets must be realized before implementing downstream projects.

- During a budget crisis, like our current one, **the president should issue a quarterly, audited financial report to the people** so that they may know that the results of the debt-reduction plan are being achieved on schedule. (This is standard operating procedure for any major firm.)

- Before being implemented by Congress, **all major new programs, such as health-care reform, must first be presented to the American people in detail** and then tested in suitable pilot programs to prove their suitability and cost-effectiveness.

- **Emulate the success of other countries.** We look to the accomplishments of foreign governments with envy, especially Germany and Japan, both of whom suffered horrendous defeats at our hands in World War II, and who now possess economies that rival and exceed ours in virtually every respect. How did they do it? They did it partially through American aid and know-how and partially through American disinterest and self-absorption. Are these countries better than we are? Not really. They just got in tune with the times: They established a longterm strategic plan, employed realistic quality-control programs with "teeth," and insisted—no *demanded*—day-to-day cost effectiveness. They didn't pass more taxes to feed government inefficiency. After all, government will consume all that it is given. These countries learned how to save from within. They streamlined and reformed. They did **not** regulate themselves into irrelevancy—they got smart!

WE MUST MANAGE SMARTER

Because little or no cost accounting is used in our Congress, it is virtually impossible to determine the cost versus the benefits of various programs. Furthermore, no sales or marketing functions exist, with perhaps the exception of military recruitment, to promote legitimate government programs. Thus private citizens, businesses, and even other governments have no way of determining the existence of programs of value to themselves. It becomes exclusively an insider's game. Why else are the major businesses in Washington all consultants?

Virtually no strategic planning function covers government operations. No mission statements or critical issues are developed. No one ever asks, "How can we do it better, or perhaps even less expensively?" There is no ongoing program to evaluate the useful life of any project. Has it accomplished its purpose? Is it still cost-effective? No, after most programs are enacted, they are immortal—funded year after year, irrespective of their true value to the nation.

These poor management practices have been reviewed in countless studies and government reports. Unfortunately, the tendency of the majority of these studies is to propose broad-based major structural and programmatic changes that in the current climate are politically infeasible and therefore never implemented. The practical proposals intertwined in these broad recommendations are invariably lost in the political debate because their priorities invariably conflict with the legislators' sole priority of reelection at all costs.

Thus nothing substantive has been done to overhaul government management practices. Even comprehensive recommendations by such prestigious groups as the

Grace Commission and other mandated public organizations are thrown on the slag heap of political expediency.

Despite the public perception to the contrary, most government bureaucrats are actually competent people. That's right—government executives are in fact quite good and extremely rational in their actions. The problem is incorrect incentives.

The legislative branch's version of solutions to poor management practices is to impose more regulations and more requirements, which has exactly the opposite effect.

Adding to the overwhelming volume of regulations is not the answer. By overregulating the decision-making process and choices, the legislative branch has removed any semblance of common sense from the process. This "micromanagement" system is costly and inefficient, and does not produce the best results. How else do you obtain $600 toilet seats and $75 light bulbs that you can buy in any corner store for $1.25?

The answer surely is not in more taxes.

Simply put, government managers do not need new "make-work" laws that require them to create more reports or perform additional studies. They need the tools and incentives to streamline their own operations and to save the taxpayers' money.

Congressional proposals aside, the new administration must place a higher priority on the *management* of government and *the qualifications of the people who are appointed to serve.* This prioritizing cannot be done with political appointees who have never managed anything successfully in their lives. It must be done by appointing people with a track record of running something complex and successful. They are out there, and they are willing to serve.

ELIMINATING THE PRIVILEGED CLASS

First and foremost, America's privileged class must be eliminated.

The reform of Congress must have as its objective a return to the original operating concepts of our Founding Fathers. By cleansing the present institution of the corruption insidiously inserted by decades of self-serving political hacks who placed greed and personal self-aggrandizement above duty to country, and by eliminating life tenure and personal political fiefdoms, we can sieze it from the privileged class and return the United States Congress to all the people.

Unrealistic? Hardly. What man can corrupt, man can cleanse.

America has no place for class distinctions—not on our city streets and not in our Congress. Every taxpayer and every citizen lives here on an equal basis. Special privilege has no place in our government. Those who serve must do so willingly and with no thought of special favors or preferred positions. Our citizen legislators can have but one priority: to serve the national interests and enable our citizens to live in conformity with the dreams and ideals established by our Founding Fathers.

Only when our citizens impose the reality of these reforms and the Congress responds will the Congress receive the love, respect, and support given to a body dedicated to benefiting the welfare of all its citizens without respect to class.

11

Conclusion

___

According to Webster, one definition of politics is "the plotting or scheming of those seeking personal power, glory, position or the like." Disraeli considered politics as "this career of plundering and blundering . . .[where] nothing is contemptible." Shakespeare's Hamlet perceptively observed, "Something is rotten in Denmark." How very true.

Plain speakers such as Harry Truman considered politics to be the art of government; some, like James A. ("Big Jim") Farley, considered politics a science. However, others, including Otto von Bismarck, were quick to point out that "politics are not an exact science."

However, plain folks—the electorate, if you will—view politics and politicians in a somewhat different light. Because hope springs eternal (naively, perhaps), they subscribe to the proposition that the end of all political effort must be the well-being of the individual in a life of safety and freedom and that those who champion these objectives through the political process are the saviors of mankind.

Politicians are raised to positions of high honor and prestige, given the title of "the Honorable," and ultimately are confused with the position itself, especially when in the course of political events their immediate successes are attained by saying what people can be made to believe rather than what is demonstrably true. The accent is generally placed more on the desirable rather than on the possible.

In the end, when our system—as it eventually must—corrupts the incorruptible, when our champions' feet of clay crumble in the muck and mire of political expediency, we fault only the politicians and then abandon them to the ages and pour ridicule and censure on their careers. We rebuke the very actions that merited our praise and approbation such a short time before.

We take the attitude that our government is now so huge and affects our lives so directly that we cannot be content with merely a moderately decent level of behavior on the part of our public officials—that what once could be tolerated when government was small cannot be endured when government is big.

In the end, we always fault the politician, never the system. And it is the system that is truly at fault.

Any system created by man is imperfect, and although we like to think that our Founding Fathers created a perfect model, even they in their superb wisdom could not incorporate into that model sufficient safeguards to protect it from the tinkering and fiddling of modern politicians. As Disraeli observed, "In politics experiments mean resolutions." Resolutions mean votes, and votes lead to reelection.

It has been said that "the purification of politics is an iridescent dream," a nebulous objective as unobtainable as a Holy Grail. Yet purify it we must if we are to survive as a modern nation.

Politics is the science of necessities, and it will be only through the exercise of this science that effective control of our government will be returned to the citizens of the United States. The political crucible of necessity can fire a new Congress whose first priorities are matters of national interest.

The 103rd Congress is thrice blessed. It has 110 new members, the greatest turnover in legislators since Eisenhower was swept into office. It is composed of the highest majority of freshmen politicians uncorrupted by the political process ever to grace the halls of Congress. And its members were elected with a clear mandate from the people: *Change the way Congress is behaving, and bring about congressional reform.*

I believe the 103rd Congress will fail in this objective. Expecting politicians (even brand-spanking new ones) to improve a system to the betterment of the people (and perhaps even to the opposing party) while simultaneously voting to reduce or eliminate their own special privileges and benefits is similar to asking a leopard to change its spots—it cannot be done.

The people must act in spite of the politicians. By employing the political process, the people must vote to change the system and incorporate changes and limitations on the Congress that the people believe will improve the performance of the Congress. The people must put aside regional self-interest and the self-aggrandizement of politicians and replace it with the self-interest of the nation. The people must effect such changes as are necessary to eliminate America's privileged class.

While accomplishing all of this, the people must bear in mind today's perception of a politician: **Professional politicians are cheats and liars, and when they are not kissing babies, they are stealing their lollipops.**

Remember, and act accordingly.

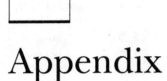

Appendix

These figures include the congressional pay raise of 1991, which established base salaries at $125,500. They incorporate the 1992 COLAs of 3.2 percent, which raised 1993 salaries to $133,600.

The estimated lifetime benefits take into consideration length of federal service, age at retirement, and life expectancy at retirement based on standard mortality tables and COLAs conservatively estimated at 4 percent per year. These benefits may be higher if Social Security income is included.

Because congressional vesting occurs after five years, only members elected before 1984 are included in these computations.

Senator	Year Born (19–)	Age Benefits Begin	Estimated Initial $ Benefits	Estimated Lifetime Benefits
Adams	27	66	62,299	1,718,477
Akaka	24	71	54,778	1,124,088
Baucus	41	56	80,301	3,765,030
Bentsen	21	74	100,201	1,720,370
Biden	42	55	75,517	3,673,283
Bingaman	43	60	36,609	1,282,030
Boren	41	56	56,542	2,651,045
Bradley	43	54	54,783	2,838,475
Breaux*	44	55	97,509	4,580,103
Bumpers*	25	74	92,391	1,299,401
Burdick	8	87	100,714	798,073
Byrd	17	78	111,795	1,507,702
Chafee	22	73	90,511	1,649,480
Coats	43	62	47,300	1,415,621
Cochran	37	60	84,938	3,239,077
Cohen	40	57	84,234	3,753,192
Cranston	14	79	63,624	807,679
D'Amato*	37	62	61,684	1,962,352
Danforth	36	59	54,233	2,180,063
Daschle*	47	52	76,184	4,190,970
DeConcini	37	58	56,656	298,174
Dixon	27	66	33,318	913,025
Dodd*	44	55	107,323	5,041,080
Dole	23	70	103,978	2,261,645
Domenici	32	55	78,425	2,273,456
Durenberger	34	61	54,778	1,979,485
Exon	21	76	68,656	1,045,654
Ford*	24	75	88,879	1,157,291
Fowler*	40	59	95,703	3,614,168
Garn	32	61	56,197	2,024,414
Glenn*	21	78	112,907	1,133,885
Gore	42	55	62,143	3,063,288
Gorton	28	67	36,609	947,592
Gramm	42	55	55,955	2,758,290

Senator	Year Born (19–)	Age Benefits Begin	Estimated Initial $ Benefits	Estimated Lifetime Benefits
Grassley*	33	66	82,155	2,045,353
Harkin	39	58	86,436	3,658,748
Hatch	34	61	54,778	1,979,485
Hatfield	22	75	104,477	1,689,619
Heflin	21	76	71,912	1,095,251
Helms	21	76	96,336	1,467,230
Hollings*	22	77	112,907	1,239,232
Inouye*	24	75	112,907	1,468,505
Jeffords	34	61	72,342	2,614,175
Johnston	32	65	88,194	2,556,660
Kassebaum	32	65	70,557	2,580,227
Kasten*	42	57	76,389	3,221,388
Kennedy	32	63	111,605	3,617,992
Lautenberg	24	71	48,722	998,805
Leahy*	40	59	81,336	3,071,609
Levin	34	63	58,886	1,908,966
Lott	41	54	74,901	3,880,821
Lugar	32	63	63,863	2,070,292
Mack	40	62	36,609	1,151,623
McCain*	36	63	54,860	1,644,257
Metzenbaum	17	78	54,778	738,756
Mikulski*	36	63	83,402	3,261,650
Mitchell	33	62	87,419	2,991,898
Moynihan	27	68	79,610	1,944,760
Murkowski*	33	66	65,096	1,620,638
Nickles*	48	51	70,916	4,107,346
Nunn	38	59	77,644	3,121,121
Packwood*	32	67	102,693	2,392,945
Pell	18	79	108,285	1,374,633
Pressler	42	55	74,517	3,673,283
Pryor	34	63	78,425	2,542,371
Reid*	34	65	54,860	1,455,275
Riegle	38	57	82,517	3,676,681
Roth	21	74	94,145	1,616,386

Senator	Year Born (19–)	Age Benefits Begin	Estimated Initial $ Benefits	Estimated Lifetime Benefits
Rudman	30	63	35,860	1,162,508
Sarbanes	33	62	79,004	2,703,888
Sasser	36	59	54,233	2,180,063
Shelby*	34	65	73,967	1,962,114
Simon	28	69	78,425	1,810,846
Simpson	31	66	65,399	1,792,158
Specter*	30	69	68,503	1,396,060
Stevens	23	74	108,285	1,859,155
Symms	38	55	55,816	2,742,802
Thurmond	02	95	108,285	554,369
Wallop	33	62	60,835	2,082,046
Warner	27	70	108,187	2,353,187
Wirth	39	54	47,405	2,456,205

* Assuming reelection in 1992

Congressperson	Year Born (19–)	Age Benefits Begin	Estimated Initial $ Benfits	Estimated Lifetime Benefits
Ackerman	42	60	25,574	907,650
Alexander	34	59	67,977	2,731,658
Anderson	13	80	68,661	820,101
Andrews	44	60	26,574	894,756
Annunzio	15	78	73,996	997,936
Anthony	38	60	37,096	1,337,413
Applegate	28	65	42,357	1,189,639
Archer	28	65	63,400	1,780,667
Aspin	38	55	74,134	3,589,987
AuCoin	42	51	48,328	2,898,360
Barnard	22	71	47,618	976,831
Bartlett	47	60	26,574	879,543
Bateman	28	65	31,835	894,125
Bates	41	60	37,096	1,276,509

Congressperson	Year Born (19–)	Age Benefits Begin	Estimated Initial $ Benfits	Estimated Lifetime Benefits
Beilenson	32	61	42,357	1,494,325
Bennett	10	83	93,634	933,952
Bereuter	39	60	45,514	1,593,874
Berman	41	60	26,574	914,447
Bevill	21	72	71,292	1,299,225
Bilirakis	30	63	37,096	1,169,421
Bliley	32	61	39,727	1,401,525
Boehlert	36	57	70,437	3,077,341
Bonior*	45	50	49,686	3,057,666
Borski	48	60	26,574	875,310
Bosco	46	60	29,227	972,009
Boucher	46	60	29,227	972,009
Boxer	40	60	33,150	1,517,218
Brooks	22	71	93,634	1,822,301
Broomfield	22	71	93,634	1,918,896
Brown	20	73	95,083	1,624,635
Bryant	47	60	26,574	879,543
Burton	38	60	29,205	1,032,398
Byron	32	61	37,096	1,665,059
Carper	47	60	39,727	1,328,936
Carr	43	60	48,225	1,634,838
Chandler	42	60	26,574	922,214
Clay	31	62	63,400	2,115,769
Clinger	29	64	52,879	1,573,492
Coleman, T.	43	60	44,987	1,525,095
Coleman, R.	41	60	31,835	1,095,478
Collins	31	62	58,454	2,483,579
Conte	21	72	93,634	1,706,383
Conyers	29	64	101,710	3,026,551
Cooper	54	60	26,574	856,107
Coughlin	29	64	66,031	2,024,239
Coyne	36	60	40,918	1,475,686
Crane	30	63	68,661	2,164,486
Dannemeyer	29	64	42,357	1,298,493

Congressperson	Year Born (19–)	Age Benefits Begin	Estimated Initial $ Benfits	Estimated Lifetime Benefits
Darden	43	60	26,574	900,883
Davis	32	61	37,096	1,340,079
de la Garza	27	66	79,183	2,095,692
Dellums	35	58	62,138	2,576,435
Derrick	36	57	46,197	2,018,334
Dickinson	25	68	81,814	1,997,939
Dicks	40	53	56,522	3,028,459
Dingell	26	67	93,634	2,332,953
Dixon	34	60	44,987	1,657,147
Donnelly	46	60	37,096	1,248,609
Dorgan	42	60	31,835	1,087,336
Downey	49	50	40,516	2,470,574
Dreier	52	60	35,072	1,136,974
Durbin	44	60	26,574	894,756
Dwyer	21	72	44,987	819,853
Dymally	26	67	31,835	823,763
Dyson	48	60	39,457	1,299,625
Early	33	60	52,879	2,015,843
Eckart	50	60	31,835	1,048,248
Edwards, D.	15	78	90,231	1,100,391
Edwards, M.	37	60	42,357	1,543,358
Emerson	38	55	53,997	2,614,807
English	40	53	43,357	2,323,057
Erdreich	38	60	31,835	1,147,745
Fascell	17	76	93,634	1,424,195
Fazio	42	60	37,096	1,267,022
Feighan	47	60	26,574	888,969
Fields	52	60	35,072	1,136,974
Fish	26	67	81,836	2,039,003
Foglietta	28	65	35,580	1,083,551
Foley	29	64	102,701	3,059,249
Ford, H.	45	50	40,516	2,493,325
Ford, W.	27	66	87,681	3,320,607
Frost	42	60	39,200	1,338,896

Congressperson	Year Born (19–)	Age Benefits Begin	Estimated Initial $ Benfits	Estimated Lifetime Benefits
Gaydos	26	67	68,661	1,776,665
Gejdenson	48	60	31,835	1,048,594
Gekas	30	63	31,835	1,003,577
Gephardt	41	60	47,067	1,622,893
Gibbons	20	73	92,235	1,577,687
Gilman	22	71	58,140	1,131,516
Gingrich	43	60	37,096	1,257,575
Glickman	44	60	45,514	1,532,435
Gonzalez	16	77	84,444	1,103,347
Goodling	27	66	52,879	1,399,510
Gradison	28	65	57,087	1,603,359
Gray	41	60	37,096	1,276,509
Green	29	64	62,874	1,927,472
Guarini	24	69	46,763	1,079,413
Gunderson	51	60	35,781	1,163,972
Hall, R.	23	70	39,727	822,325
Hall, T.	42	60	37,096	1,267,022
Hamilton	31	62	73,922	2,466,896
Hammerschmidt	22	71	76,553	1,570,398
Hansen	32	61	42,357	1,494,325
Hatcher	39	60	42,357	1,511,914
Hayes	18	75	26,574	429,625
Hefner	30	63	47,618	1,501,109
Hertel	48	60	31,835	1,058,400
Hiler	53	60	34,992	1,130,421
Hopkins	33	60	42,357	1,614,734
Horton	19	74	89,705	1,539,642
Hoyer	39	60	31,835	1,114,864
Hubbard	37	56	45,724	2,143,131
Huckaby	41	60	42,357	1,482,843
Hughes	32	61	47,618	1,679,925
Hunter	48	60	37,096	1,221,877
Hutto	26	67	52,357	1,055,357
Hyde	24	69	52,879	1,165,735

Congressperson	Year Born (19–)	Age Benefits Begin	Estimated Initial $ Benfits	Estimated Lifetime Benefits
Ireland	30	63	42,357	1,372,668
Jacobs	32	61	31,564	1,819,125
Jenkins	33	60	63,400	2,416,952
Johnson	46	60	26,574	1,192,062
Jones	13	80	71,292	754,467
Kaptur	46	60	37,411	1,678,152
Kasich	52	60	29,227	947,479
Kastenmeier	24	69	93,634	2,064,193
Kennelly	36	60	29,205	1,361,096
Kildee	29	64	42,357	1,260,400
Kleczka	43	62	23,944	705,311
Kolter	26	67	34,466	891,827
Kostmayer	46	60	37,096	1,248,609
LaFalce	39	54	51,153	2,605,957
Lagomarsino	26	67	55,509	1,436,343
Lantos	28	65	38,937	1,093,597
Leach	42	51	48,557	2,874,384
Lehman, R.	48	60	26,574	875,310
Lehman, W.	13	80	93,634	631,591
Lent	31	62	58,140	1,989,155
Levin	31	62	26,574	886,825
Levine	43	60	33,150	1,140,360
Lewis, J.	34	60	37,096	1,366,465
Lewis, T.	24	69	52,353	1,154,137
Lipinski	37	60	26,574	948,874
Livingston	43	50	46,776	2,908,869
Lloyd	29	64	52,609	1,565,457
Lowery	47	60	31,835	1,064,956
Madigan	36	57	51,300	2,241,283
Markey	46	60	49,686	1,652,415
Marlenee	35	60	42,357	1,577,253
Martin	44	60	42,357	1,446,229
Martinez	29	64	37,096	1,103,854
Matsui	41	60	37,096	1,276,509

Congressperson	Year Born (19–)	Age Benefits Begin	Estimated Initial $ Benfits	Estimated Lifetime Benefits
Mavroules	29	64	37,096	1,137,216
Mazzol	32	61	63,400	2,236,725
McCandless	27	66	37,096	981,801
McCloskey	39	60	37,096	1,299,099
McCollum	44	60	39,727	1,337,588
McCurdy	50	60	31,835	1,039,213
McDade	31	62	82,340	2,747,797
McEwen	50	60	31,835	1,048,248
McGrath	42	60	31,835	1,104,782
McHugh	38	55	45,250	2,229,856
Michel	23	70	104,118	2,158,947
Miller, C.	17	76	68,661	1,045,394
Miller, G.	45	50	40,616	2,493,325
Mineta	31	62	55,509	1,852,242
Moakley	27	66	60,770	1,608,365
Mollohan	43	60	26,574	900,883
Montgomery	20	73	87,681	1,498,165
Moody	35	60	35,072	1,305,997
Moorhead	22	71	60,770	1,182,710
Morrison	33	60	37,096	1,414,179
Mrazek	45	60	35,781	1,212,588
Murphy	27	66	47,618	1,260,274
Murtha	32	61	60,770	2,143,925
Myers	27	66	71,292	1,886,838
Natcher	9	84	93,634	740,754
Neal	34	59	47,144	1,853,209
Nowak	35	58	51,827	2,193,041
Oaker	40	60	46,763	2,157,749
Oberstar	34	59	77,092	3,030,422
Obey	38	55	60,244	2,917,334
Olin	20	73	34,466	627,897
Ortiz	37	60	35,072	1,252,311
Owens	37	60	29,227	1,043,593
Packard	31	62	31,835	1,062,390

Congressperson	Year Born (19–)	Age Benefits Begin	Estimated Initial $ Benfits	Estimated Lifetime Benefits
Panetta	38	55	56,995	2,760,020
Parris	29	64	43,672	1,299,537
Pashayan	41	60	47,618	1,638,572
Pease	31	62	47,618	1,629,170
Penny	51	60	26,574	864,479
Perkins	54	62	23,944	672,269
Petri	40	60	42,357	1,470,040
Pickle	13	80	93,634	990,905
Porter	35	60	39,727	1,447,992
Pursell	32	61	47,618	1,720,171
Quillen	16	77	89,705	1,172,085
Rahall	49	60	56,993	1,868,183
Rangel	30	63	73,922	2,330,331
Ray	27	66	56,824	1,556,664
Regula	24	69	58,140	1,281,713
Richardson	47	60	41,042	1,358,377
Ridge	45	60	31,835	1,065,307
Rinaldo	31	62	58,454	1,999,913
Ritter	40	60	37,096	1,310,925
Roberts	36	57	75,540	3,300,289
Roe	24	69	75,990	1,754,046
Rogers	37	60	31,835	1,136,721
Rose, C.	39	54	49,196	2,506,257
Rostenkowski	28	65	93,634	2,629,795
Roth	38	60	37,096	1,311,358
Roukema	29	64	31,835	1,209,301
Rowland	26	67	31,835	793,200
Roybal	16	77	81,814	1,172,899
Russo	44	50	40,516	2,533,986
Sabo	38	60	37,096	1,311,358
Savage	25	68	43,841	1,070,615
Saxton	43	62	23,944	705,311
Schaefer	36	60	31,835	1,148,124
Scheuer	20	73	80,498	1,466,519

Congressperson	Year Born (19–)	Age Benefits Begin	Estimated Initial $ Benfits	Estimated Lifetime Benefits
Schroeder	40	53	52,931	3,605,967
Schulze	29	64	52,879	1,621,046
Schumer	50	60	31,835	1,039,213
Sensenbrenner	43	60	37,096	1,257,575
Sharp	42	51	54,049	3,199,510
Shaw	39	60	31,835	1,114,864
Shuster	32	61	58,140	2,051,125
Sikorski	48	60	26,574	883,497
Sisisky	27	66	29,205	772,946
Skeen	27	66	34,466	912,183
Skelton	31	62	42,357	1,413,516
Slattery	48	60	26,574	875,310
Smith, B.	31	62	26,574	886,827
Smith, C.	53	60	31,835	1,028,449
Smith, D.	38	60	49,196	1,739,096
Smith, L.	41	60	26,574	930,323
Smith, N	20	73	93,634	1,599,870
Snowe	47	60	40,918	1,830,998
Solarz	40	53	43,357	2,358,547
Solomon	30	63	39,727	1,252,343
Spence	28	65	63,400	1,780,667
Spratt	42	60	31,835	1,087,336
Stangeland	30	63	42,357	1,335,265
Stark	31	62	64,300	2,145,773
Stenholm	38	60	37,096	1,311,358
Stokes	25	68	71,292	1,671,782
Studds	37	56	65,936	3,034,247
Stump	27	66	55,531	1,469,718
Sundquist	36	60	31,835	1,148,124
Swift	35	60	51,564	1,879,437
Synar	50	60	40,918	1,335,703
Tallon	46	60	26,574	894,461
Tauzin	43	60	34,466	1,168,402
Thomas, L.	43	60	37,096	1,276,088

Congressperson	Year Born (19–)	Age Benefits Begin	Estimated Initial $ Benfits	Estimated Lifetime Benefits
Thomas, W.	41	60	26,574	914,447
Torres	30	63	37,096	1,169,421
Torricelli	51	60	33,940	1,104,074
Towns	34	60	31,835	1,172,676
Traxler	31	62	55,509	1,899,158
Udall	22	71	93,634	1,822,301
Valentine	26	67	31,835	793,200
Vander Jagt	31	62	71,292	2,439,135
Vento	40	60	42,357	1,470,404
Volkmer	31	62	47,618	1,589,080
Vucanovich	21	72	42,357	993,265
Walgren	40	60	42,357	1,470,404
Walker	42	51	59,770	3,538,183
Waxman	39	54	44,304	2,257,007
Weber	52	60	42,379	1,253,465
Weiss	27	66	44,987	1,190,655
Wheat	51	60	35,072	1,140,927
Whitten	10	83	93,634	796,855
Williams	37	60	43,672	1,559,376
Wilson	33	60	63,400	2,361,633
Wise	48	60	26,574	875,310
Wolf*	39	54	46,994	1,394,094
Wolpe	39	60	48,225	1,721,353
Wyden	49	60	35,072	1,149,651
Wylie	20	73	73,922	1,346,716
Yates	19	74	93,634	1,497,665
Yatron	27	66	63,400	1,736,811
Young, C.	30	63	67,346	2,123,025
Young, D.	33	60	52,879	1,969,704

Note: The estimated lifetime pension benefits for Representatives Bonior and Wolf may be affected by other federal service dates, which are unclear from official congressional biographies.

Selected Bibliography

Activities and Summary Report of the Committee on the District of Columbia. House of Representatives, Washington, D.C. U.S. Government Printing Office, House Report 101-1023, 1991.

Governance of the Nation's Capital. House of Representatives, Washington, D.C. U.S. Government Printing Office, #-S-2, 1990.

Indices: A Statistical Index to District of Columbia Services. Library of Congress Cat. #ISSN 09895-027X, 1990.

Reilly, Claire. *Feathering Thier Own Nests.* Congressional Accountability Project, Washington, D.C., 1991.

Van Deek, Stephen D. "Let the House and Senate Judge One Another's Ethics." *Los Angeles Times.* 18 March 1992.

INDEX